The Voyages of

COLUMBUS

Rex and Thea Rienits

The Voyages of
COLUMBUS
Rex and Thea Rienits

CRESCENT BOOKS
New York

Color Plates

This 1989 edition published by Crescent Books,
distributed by Crown Publishers, Inc.
225 Park Avenue South
New York, New York 10003

First published in Great Britain by
The Hamlyn Publishing Group Limited
Michelin House, 81 Fulham Road
London SW3 6RB

© Copyright The Hamlyn Publishing Group Limited 1970

ISBN 0-517-69039-X

Produced by Mandarin Offset

Printed and bound in Hong Kong

CONTENTS

PRE-COLUMBIAN AMERICA

Little is known for certain about the first inhabitants of America. There is a widely-accepted theory that they came from Asia in the remote past by way of the Aleutian Islands or across what is now Bering Strait when it was still an isthmus linking the two continents, and that from present Alaska they gradually spread south and east seeking a more hospitable climate and better hunting grounds, until in time the whole of north, central and south America were occupied. If this theory is correct, the Eskimos of the far north and the Terra del Fuegans of the far south and all the aboriginal peoples in between – the North American Indians, the now-extinct Mayans, Toltecs and Incas, and the present-day Indians of the Amazon basin and further south – are all of common stock; modern anthropological research tends to support this view.

Even less certainty exists regarding the first Europeans who set foot on American soil. There is a persistent tradition that Phoenician traders reached South America as early as 450 B.C. Certainly the Phoenicians were the most adventurous seafarers of their time, and their ships were of a size and a seaworthiness to make long ocean voyages possible.

The Greek historian Herodotus recounts, for instance, that about 600 B.C. a fleet manned by Phoenicians circumnavigated Africa – a voyage of nearly 20,000 miles – in less than three years, sailing west-about from the Arabian Gulf and putting in at a convenient spot each autumn to sow and harvest enough grain to see them through the following year. Herodotus accepted the story as true with one important reservation. The Phoenician voyagers had declared firmly that while they were rounding the south coast of Africa, sailing west, they had had the sun on their right, and this he flatly refused to believe.

In view of the times in which he lived Herodotus's scepticism is understandable, but far from throwing doubt on the authenticity of the voyage this claim, in the light of modern knowledge, tends to suggest that in fact it did take place.

About a century and a half later, again on the authority of Herodotus, a Carthaginian named Sataspes tried to make the same voyage in reverse, sailing through the Straits of Gibraltar and then down the west African coast. However, he turned back after some months saying that further progress was impossible, and as a penalty for his failure he was impaled by order of the Persian king, Xerxes.

From the account of Herodotus it seems likely that Sataspes passed Cape Verde, the westernmost point of Africa, and got as far as the Guinea coast. Both he and the Phoenicians would thus, at one point, have been within about a thousand miles of the eastern tip of what is now Brazil. As the sea between is largely an area of doldrums, which would present no problems to ships powered by oars as well as sails, and as the prevailing wind, when there is any, is from the south-east, there is no practical reason why the tradition should not be true.

Certainly in the fourth century B.C. the Greek scholar Theopompus is on record as having written that far

The monument to Columbus at Barcelona.

beyond Africa and the known limits of the world there lay an island 'of immense extent'; and while it is easy to dismiss this as an inspired guess there is at least a possibility that the statement was based on knowledge.

According to another tradition a Benedictine abbot, St Brendan, with a crew of monks, crossed the Atlantic from Ireland some time in the sixth century A.D. in a large curragh equipped with sail and oars. The first account of this voyage appeared in an anonymous manuscript of the eleventh century titled *Navigatio Brendani*. It gave circumstantial details of St Brendan's adventures and stated that he had reached 'the promised land of the saints', which some believed to be the mainland of North America and some the island of Madeira.

Although the story was widely accepted until the seventeenth century and St Brendan's Land, variously located, appeared on many maps, most modern scholars dismiss it as legend. However, the line between legend and truth is sometimes thin. It has been established, for instance, that there were Irish settlers in Iceland as early as A.D. 850, and presumably they got there by curragh; and the fact that as recently as 1966 two men crossed the north Atlantic in a rowing boat suggests that St Brendan's voyage, although perhaps unlikely, was at least feasible.

Another story dismissed as legend is that of the Welsh prince Madoc ap Owen Gwyneth. According to one version of this, when Madoc's father died his elder brothers quarrelled over who should succeed him, and rather than become involved Madoc took ship from Wales about 1170 and sailed to the south of Ireland and then westward until he reached what is now Florida. Years later, the story continues, Madoc returned home, recruited a number of Welsh men and women, and then sailed back with them to establish a colony in America.

Yet another legend concerns Henry Sinclair, a Scot of mixed Norman and Norwegian blood and first prince of the Orkneys, who supposedly led an expedition to Nova Scotia in 1398 and founded a settlement there. The evidence for this is based on letters from two Venetian seamen, Nicolo and Antonio Zeno, to their brother Carlo, which were published by a descendant in 1558. In these the brothers claimed that they had successfully navigated several ships from the Orkneys to an unknown land in the distant west, but the references to its location are vague, and there is even doubt as to the authenticity of the letters themselves.

Lacking proof it is easy to dismiss these stories. Yet there could be some element of truth in them, for the myth of the Atlantic as a graveyard for mariners has long since been exploded. Today single-handed yacht crossings are so commonplace that they barely get a mention in the newspapers. In 1966 two members of the Special Air Services Regiment, Captain J. Ridgway and Sergeant C. Blyth, rowed from Cape Cod to Ireland in 91 days; in 1969 another member of the same unit, Trooper Tom McClean, did even better by rowing alone from Newfoundland to Ireland in 72 days. In the same year John Fairfax rowed and drifted from the Canary Islands to Florida in about six months, while the Norwegian

Thor Heyerdahl travelled most of the way across from Morocco to Barbados in a papyrus boat built on the lines of ancient Egyptian river-craft. The best ships of medieval times, although primitive by modern standards, were certainly more seaworthy than any of the above, and the greatest deterrent to seamen of that time was not the Atlantic itself but their terror of the unknown.

Even if Madoc and Sinclair did in fact establish settlements in America, however, they were not the first Europeans to do so, for the Norsemen had preceded Madoc by almost two centuries and Sinclair by four.

The sagas which described the voyages and adventures of these Norsemen were also dismissed for many years as legends, but modern research and archaeology have proved their accuracy and it is now accepted without question that there were Norse colonists in America almost a thousand years ago.

The first Norsemen known to have made contact with America were Bjarni Herjulfsson and his crew, who sailed from Iceland in the summer of 985 A.D. intending to join Bjarni's father at Herjulfness, a newly-established colony in Greenland. After having been driven south by adverse winds they were fog-bound for several days, and when the weather cleared they found themselves off a long shoreline of forests and low hills.

Bjarni realized he had gone beyond Greenland, and refusing his crew's request to land for water and wood, he turned his ship north. Two other stretches of coast were seen – the first flat and heavy-timbered, the second mountainous and ice-bound. Then with a favourable wind Bjarni turned east away from the land and a few days later reached Herjulfness. From the saga which describes Bjarni's voyage it is not certain whether his first landfall was Nova Scotia or Newfoundland, but his second was undoubtedly Labrador and his third Baffin Land, from whence he sailed across Davis Strait and back to Greenland.

For some years nothing was done to follow up this discovery. Then Leif Eiriksson, whose father Eirik the Red had founded the Greenland colony, bought Bjarni's ship, and in 1002 he set out to follow Bjarni's route in reverse. After reaching the coast and sailing south for some time Leif went ashore briefly at what he called Markland, which means wood or forest land. Historians are fairly sure that his landing point was on the Labrador coast near Sandwich Bay. Some distance farther south Leif found more hospitable land, thickly timbered, with lush green pastures, plentiful fish and flourishing grapevines. He named it Vinland (or Vineland) and found it so congenial that he wintered at a spot he called Leifsbudir. The following spring he returned to Greenland with a cargo of timber and grapes.

For many years scholars have argued over the whereabouts of Vinland. Books have been written to prove it was in Newfoundland, in Nova Scotia, at Falmouth on Cape Cod, on Rhode Island, on the site of New York, and even as far south as Florida. Since 1962 a team of Norwegian archaeologists led by Dr Helge Ingstad has uncovered evidence of Norse occupation at L'Anseaux Meadows on the northern promontory of Newfoundland,

An artist's impression of the first landing of the
Norse adventurer Leif Eiriksson on American soil.

above, left:
St Brendan and his sea-going monks celebrate
Mass on the back of a benign sea-monster. St
Brendan's island is vaguely located at the top.
From a book published in Venice in 1621.

and it is nowadays widely but by no means unanimously
agreed that this was the site of Leif's settlement. Certainly grapes do not grow there today, and in fact their
present northern limit is about three hundred miles to
the south. But in the fifteen-thirties when the Frenchman Jacques Cartier discovered the St Lawrence River,
which is in about the same latitude as Newfoundland, he
found grapes growing abundantly on both banks, and
this suggests that the climate generally was milder then
than now. Unless and until other demonstrably Norse
remains are found in America it is difficult to contest Dr
Ingstad's belief that Vinland and Newfoundland are the
same country.

Leif Eiriksson's voyage had been so successful that in
the following year his brother Thorvald also visited
Labrador and wintered in Vinland. A year later he
returned to Labrador and discovered and sailed up a
scenically beautiful fjord, almost certainly the present
Hamilton Inlet. Here he and his men clashed with hostile
Indians, believed to have been Algonquins; Thorvald

was killed by a stray arrow which penetrated between
his shield and the gunwale of his ship. The following
spring when Thorvald's death was reported in Greenland another brother, Thorstein, set out to recover his
body but failed to find it. Some years ago, while excavat-
ing on Thorstein's farm in Greenland, Danish archaeologists found an arrowhead of the type used by the
Algonquins, and it is possible that Thorvald's crew may
have brought the arrow back as proof of how their leader
had met his death.

In 1010 Thorfinn Karlsefni, who is said to have been
of Irish ancestry, sailed from Greenland with three ships,
meaning to form a permanent settlement in Vinland. He
and some others were accompanied by their wives, and
they also took cattle, sheep, horses and probably goats
and pigs. It is uncertain how long they remained, but
they were so constantly harassed by hostile Indians who
destroyed their crops and killed their stock that eventually they abandoned the colony and returned to Greenland. In Vinland Karlsefni's wife, Gudrid, bore a son

A North American Indian arrowhead which may have been the one that killed the Norseman Thorvald Eiriksson. It was found on his brother Thorstein's farm in Greenland, where the North American Indians have never settled.

named Snorre, who may well have been the first European born on American soil.

The experience of Karlsefni and his people apparently discouraged other would-be colonists, and later records of voyages between Greenland and America are sparse. In 1121 Eirik, Bishop of Greenland, set out to find Vinland but it is not known whether he did so or even if he ever returned, and the sagas record other occasional voyages up to 1347.

Soon after Gudrid Karlsefni returned from Vinland she is said to have visited Rome. Whether this is so or not it is certain that eleventh-century ecclesiastics and scholars in Europe were well aware of the Norse voyages to America. In 1070 the German historian Adam of Bremen mentioned Vinland in his *Descriptio Insularum Aquilonis*, and about fifty years later it was again referred to by Ordericus Vitalis, a Frenchman, in his *Historia Ecclesiastica*, though neither manuscript was actually published until some centuries later.

During the first half of the fifteenth century reports of voyages far out into the Atlantic by Portuguese and Spanish ships were apparently not uncommon. No authentic written records of any seem to have survived, but several maps of the period show land well to the west of Europe. These include an anonymous map of 1424 preserved at Weimar, a map by the Genoese B. Baccario of 1434, a map by the Venetian Andrea Bianco of 1436, and others dated 1455 and 1476, in all of which the land is called Antillia. On some it is shown as a single island and on some as a group with the explanation *Insulae de novo repertae* (Newly-discovered islands). On Bianco's map there is a note *Questo he Mar de Spagna* (Here are Spanish waters).

The origin of the name Antillia is uncertain. A likely explanation is that it derives from the Latin *anterior*, signifying that it had to be passed before one could reach Cathay, and perhaps it is on this basis that sixteenth-century geographers labelled as the Greater and Lesser Antilles the island which Columbus discovered in the Caribbean.

below, left:
A Sioux painting on buffalo skin showing a chief on horseback. This – to most people – typical image of the American Indian could not have been seen by any discoverer, even before 1492. The Indians had no horses before the Spaniards came.

A valley in Peru, with the Andes soaring above. The Americas, a world of infinite variety, were visited by the white man before the time of Columbus but always from the east. The existence of the Pacific Ocean and the great continuous mountain chain were never suspected.

THE AGE OF COLUMBUS

Strictly speaking there was no such person as Christopher Columbus. The name is merely an Anglicised version of that of a man who was called Christoforo (or Cristoforo) Colombo in Italy and Cristóval (or Cristóbal) Colón in Spain. Despite centuries of research by hundreds of scholars there is still some doubt regarding where and when he was born. It has been claimed, with persuasive arguments, that he was a Castilian, a Catalan, a Corsican, a Majorcan, an Italian, a Portuguese, an Englishman, a German, a Greek and even an Armenian, and the supposed year of his birth has varied between 1436 and 1451.

All surviving letters and documents in Columbus's hand are in Spanish, but this proves nothing for they are stilted in style and may well have been written by a man for whom Spanish was an acquired language rather than his native tongue. The ambiguity of his origin and background is heightened by the fact that Columbus was a fluent and convincing liar when it suited him, particularly when he was trying to promote his first historic voyage; many statements he made then and later conflict so much that it is impossible all could be true.

There is no evidence, for instance, to support his claim that he was of noble lineage and that at least one ancestor had been an admiral; and it seems very unlikely, as his son Ferdinand stated, that he was ever a student at the University of Pavia, for apart from other presumptive evidence there is no mention of him in the matriculation rolls there. On the contrary, all the known evidence suggests that he was of comparatively humble birth and

that his schooling was slight, and it is possible that until early manhood he was illiterate.

It is generally accepted that Columbus was Italian – or rather Genoese, which in those days was somewhat different – and that his grandfather was Giovanni Colombo, who first lived at Terra Rossa, a village in the hills behind Genoa, and then at Quinto, another village on the coast five miles from the same city. Of Giovanni Colombo it is known only that he was alive in 1440 and dead in 1444, and that he had two sons, Antonio and Domenico, and one daughter, Battistina. As the elder son, Antonio inherited his father's small estates. Domenico became a wool-weaver, and also kept a tavern and bought and sold land. In about 1450 – though some give the year as 1445 – he married Susanna Fontana-Rossa, the daughter of a silk-weaver.

Soon after their marriage the Colombos bought and settled in a house, which has since disappeared, in a suburb of Genoa outside the Porta dell'Olivella (Olive Gate). Later they moved closer in to No. 37 Vico Dritto di Ponticello near the Porta Sant'Andrea (St Andrew's Gate), which is the one closest to the waterfront of Genoa. They had four sons – Christoforo, Bartolomeo, Diego and Giovanni, who died as a young man. There was one daughter, Bianchinetta, who married a cheesemonger. The eldest son, Christoforo, is thought to have been born in the first house in 1451, although no actual record of this survives, and to have lived during most of his childhood in the second, on the site of which a later house on the same foundations still stands.

House at Terra Rossa, near Genoa, where Columbus's father Domenico is thought to have been born and to have spent his childhood.

right:
The house in Vico Dritto di Ponticello, Genoa, where Columbus is believed to have spent his childhood. Apart from its foundations little of the original building now survives.

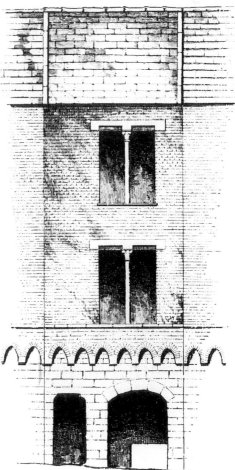

Columbus had the good fortune to be born during perhaps the most exciting period in all European history, when the movement known as the Renaissance was nearing its peak. This rebirth, as historians describe it, had begun in Italy more than a century earlier, and among the greatest of its pioneers were the poets Dante, Petrarch and Boccaccio. Basically it comprised a revival of interest in and study of classic art and letters, which had been neglected and forgotten for more than a thousand years during the period which some know as the Dark Ages. As scholars began to study the master-works of Greek and Roman literature, philosophy, political theory, history, geography, astronomy, mathematics, theology and art they became increasingly conscious of the short-comings of their own civilisation. Admiration led to emulation, and the result was a slow and often painful emergence from centuries of ecclesiastical and feudal despotism towards a new freedom of thought and expression in almost every sphere of human activity.

13

Lisbon, capital of Portugal, in the sixteenth century.

above, left:
Porta Sant'Andrea, Genoa, through which
Columbus must have passed many times during his
youth on his way to the waterfront.

In 1451, accepting this as the year of Columbus's birth, the painters Fra Angelico, Fra Filippo Lippi and Piero della Francesca, and the sculptor Donatello were still at their creative peak; the brothers Giovanni and Gentile Bellini were in their early twenties; and Sandro Botticelli and Pietro Perugino were small boys, with their years of greatness to come. In 1452, while Columbus was still in his cradle, were born two of the dominating figures of the Renaissance – Leonardo da Vinci, mathematician, engineer, inventor, architect, anatomist and artist, perhaps the most staggering genius of all time; and Girolamo Savonarola, the religious and political reformer who was to rule Florence for a time as a Christian commonwealth, and who was to suffer death at the stake.

When Columbus was two years old Constantinople fell to the Ottoman Turks, and the migration to Italy as refugees of many Greek scholars and teachers from that city gave a strong impetus to the movement: when he was four the German Johann Gutenberg produced the first book ever printed, his historic forty-two-line Bible, and

so made possible a much wider dissemination of knowledge than ever before. Erasmus, the Dutch philosopher, was born when Columbus was fifteen; Albrecht Dürer, the first great engraver, when he was twenty; Copernicus, the brilliant Polish astronomer, when he was twenty-two; and Michelangelo when he was twenty-four. Such men as the German physician Paracelsus, the Italian political philosopher Machiavelli, the painters Titian, Giorgione and Raphael, and the religious reformers Luther and Calvin also lived during his lifetime.

For Columbus, however, the most significant events of the Renaissance were taking place not in Italy but in Portugal. Here, about 1415, the young Prince Henry, a son of King John I and, through his mother, a grandson of John of Gaunt, had conceived the idea of finding a seaway down the unknown west coast of Africa and thence east to the Indies, Cathay (China) and Cipangu (Japan). In an age of religious superstition and of fear of the unknown it was a daring and, some thought, a blasphemous conception.

It was true that many centuries earlier Greek and then Arab scholars had advanced convincing theories that the world was round, but there were still a few who refused to accept this. One priestly scholar asserted that God would not permit such a thing because if the earth were round the people on the far side would not be able to see the second coming of Christ; others argued that even if the earth were round there could not be any people on the underside because men could not walk upside down, nor could there be trees or plants because rain could not fall upward to water them. Even many of those who accepted the roundness of the earth doubted whether the other side would ever be explored, for to reach it men would have to sail through the tropic zone which was well-known, they declared, to be a region 'boiling with fiery heat, peopled by fearsome sea-monsters, and threatened by the visible hand of Satan'.

Prince Henry had no such doubts. He was a practical man of science, and he believed only what could be proved. He realised that if his captains were to find a way to the Indies they would need both the best ships and thorough training in the theory and practice of navigation. So from all over Europe he engaged learned mathematicians, astronomers, geographers and map-makers and the most skilled shipwrights and makers of navigational instruments. At Sagres he established what was in effect the world's first academy of navigation.

In 1434 one of Henry's captains, Gil Eannes, groped his way cautiously down the west African coast for about 800 miles to Cape Bojador, a little way beyond the Canary Islands; and in the following year Alfonso Baldaya went about another fifty leagues to the brink of the tropics. Further voyages of discovery were postponed for a while because of a war with Morocco. Then in 1441 Antam Gonzalves got as far south as the Guinea coast, and within another five years Henry's ships were sailing regularly as far as Sierra Leone. A brisk trade had been established in gold, ivory, slaves and other commodities, and a fort had been built at Arguin to protect resident Portuguese traders. No-one denied that it was hot within the tropics, but it was not exactly boiling, and not a single sea-monster had been reliably reported.

Henry the Navigator, as later historians called him, died in 1460. He had not seen his dream of a sea-route to the Indies come true, but he had shown it was possible and he had done more to put navigation on a scientific basis than any man in history. Not all the men who had sailed in his ships were Portuguese. Among them were many Genoese, who were redoubtable seamen, and the strange and wonderful stories these men brought home could hardly have failed to stir the imagination and fire the ambition of a susceptible boy of nine as Columbus was at the time of Henry's death.

Little more is known for certain of Columbus's years of adolescence and early manhood than of his origin and birth, and again much of this ambiguity is due to his own conflicting statements and to those of his four earliest biographers, all of whom knew him personally. These were his son Ferdinand, who relied heavily on parental reminiscences; Bartholomew de las Casas, who arrived in the New World in 1502 and eight years later was the first

Gil Eannes, one of the first of Henry the Navigator's captains, who sailed down the West African coast to Cape Bojador in 1434.

priest to be ordained there; Peter Martyr, a noted scholar and lecturer who met Columbus at Barcelona on his triumphant return from his first voyage; and Gonzalo Fernández de Oviedo y Valdés, more simply known as Oviedo, who spent more than thirty years in the Caribbean and was its first noted historian.

In 1501, in a letter to his patrons, King Ferdinand and Queen Isabella of Spain, Columbus wrote: 'At a very tender age I became a sailor, and I have continued until this day . . . For forty years I have followed this trade, and I have sailed all the navigable seas'. In his journal on 21 December 1492 he wrote: 'I have followed the sea for twenty-three years without leaving it for any time worth reckoning'; and Ferdinand quotes his father as saying that he first went to sea when he was fourteen. So, on Columbus's own authority, he made his first voyage in 1461, 1465 and 1469. Most historians accept Ferdinand's version and fix the year at 1465, and it is thought that during the next eight years he sailed fairly constantly in merchantmen on the Ligurian coast.

Columbus's house in Porto Santo, near Madeira. It was here that his elder son Diego was born, probably in 1480.

The ruins of the house in which Columbus is said to have lived for a time in Funchal, Madeira.

The impression given by Columbus is that on these voyages, which rarely extended more than a hundred miles or so from his home port, he sailed before the mast. But other evidence suggests that for much of this time he was apprenticed as a wool-weaver to his father, who had now moved to Savona, on the coast west of Genoa. From this it is argued that his early years at sea were spent not as a seaman but as his father's agent, and it seems natural enough that he should have been sent by ship to buy wool, wine and cheese and to sell cloth. However, the point is not important, for in either case he would certainly have gained a good practical knowledge of seamanship and at least a working knowledge of navigation.

One of Columbus's claims which has caused much learned argument is that for some time he was at sea in the service of King René II of Anjou. His own story is that on one occasion he was sent from Marseilles to capture a galley of King Juan II of Aragon which was then at Tunis; that at San Pedro in Sardinia he learned that the galley was accompanied by three other ships; that his crew became apprehensive and demanded that he should turn back for reinforcements; and that he pretended to assent but instead changed the compass card, so that while his people thought they were on the way home in fact they found themselves next morning off the coast of Tunis.

There are three main arguments against this – first that Columbus infers he was the captain of the ship; second that some of the crew must have known enough astronomy to realize from the position of the stars that they were sailing south instead of north; and third that the ship could not have reached Tunis in a night's sail from Sardinia. One historian goes farther and asserts that if the incident occurred at all it was probably in 1459 when Columbus was aged eight.

On the other hand, most scholars accept another of Columbus's statements that in 1474, when he was aged twenty-three, he sailed in a four-masted ship, the *Roxana*, from Genoa to the Aegean island of Chios and that he stayed there until early 1475. Columbus does not say in what capacity he made the voyage, but as Chios was a Genoese colony it is possible that he took woollen goods there for his father and other merchants of Genoa.

His movements in the following year, 1476, are also shrouded in mystery. According to one account he visited Lisbon in one of a fleet of four Genoese merchantmen and spent some time there with his brother Bartholomew, who had already established himself as a bookseller and chart-maker. A second account is that the Genoese ships were attacked off Cape St Vincent by privateers; that Columbus's ship was sunk; that Columbus, although wounded, clung to an oar and swam six miles to Lagos on the south coast of Portugal; and that when he had recovered he made his way to Lisbon and joined his brother. There is historical evidence that such a battle did in fact take place on 13 August 1476, and a third and perhaps the most likely account states that Columbus was in one of the two ships which escaped and eventually reached Lisbon.

Another statement by Columbus is to the effect that after a short stay in Lisbon he continued on in the same ship to the English port of Bristol; that he went from there to Galway, Ireland; that he visited the Shetlands; and that from there in February 1477 he sailed north a hundred leagues to an island 'as large as England', which he called Tile or Thule, and which was almost certainly Iceland. There seems no particular reason to doubt this story. On the contrary, it may well have happened that while in Iceland Columbus heard some of the sagas recounting the voyages of Leif Eiriksson and other Norsemen to America, and not impossible that these first implanted in his mind the idea of sailing westward in warmer latitudes to the Indies and Cathay.

In the same year and probably in the same ship Columbus returned to Lisbon, decided to remain and joined Bartholomew in business. Unfortunately the Lisbon earthquake of 1755 destroyed many notarial and court records, some of which may have given clues to Columbus's activities there. A contemporary who knew him there described him as 'a hawker of printed books . . .

a man of great intelligence though little book-learning, very skilled in the art of cosmography and the mapping of the world', and there seems little doubt that he and Bartholomew became partners as chart-makers, booksellers and agents for Genoese exporters and that their business prospered.

By now Columbus was repairing many of the gaps in his education. In addition to his native Genoese dialect he spoke fluent Portuguese and perhaps Castilian Spanish, and familiarity with the books he sold must have taught him much Latin. He seems to have been personable and well-liked, and to have had a wide circle of friends. He was, his son wrote, '. . . a well-built man of more than medium stature, long visaged with cheeks somewhat high, but neither fat nor thin. He had an aquiline nose and his eyes were light in colour; his complexion too was light, but kindling to a vivid red. In youth his hair was blond, but when he came to his thirtieth year it all turned white. In eating and drinking and the adornment of his person he was always continent and modest. Among strangers his conversation was affable, and with members of his household very pleasant, but with a modest and pleasing dignity. In matters of religion he was so strict that for fasting and saying all the canonical offices he might have been taken for a member of a religious order'.

Columbus is thought to have returned briefly to Genoa in 1478, probably to see his family and on business affairs, and during the summer he was sent to Madeira on a sugar-buying voyage. Almost certainly in the same year he married Felipa Perestrello y Moñiz in Lisbon. His social standing at this time may be gauged by the fact that his wife and her family were very well connected. The mother, Isabel Moñiz, was distantly related to the royal house of Bragança; Felipa's father, Bartholomew Perestrello, had been one of Henry the Navigator's captains. He was also the rediscoverer and, until his death in 1457, the first governor of Porto Santo, an island about thirty miles from Madeira; and Felipa herself was a cousin of the Archbishop of Lisbon.

Perestrello's governorship was hereditary. For some time after his death the island had been administered by Pedro da Cunha, a son-in-law by an earlier marriage, but Felipa's brother, also Bartholomew, had recently come of age and had taken over.

For Columbus it was, of course, an extremely advantageous marriage. After the wedding he moved into the Moñiz family house, leaving Bartholomew to carry on the map-making business alone, and he received, probably as part of his wife's dowry, Perestrello's considerable library of books and maps. In 1479 he sailed with his wife and mother-in-law on an extended visit to Porto Santo, and here in the following year his son Diego was born.

There can be little doubt that the time he spent on the island played a big part in the shaping of his future. Porto Santo was on the very threshold of the Atlantic, that mysterious unexplored ocean, on the other side of which lay no man knew exactly what – perhaps, if the cartographers were right, the island or group called Antillia, and beyond these again Cathay and Cipangu, rich in gold and silks and spices.

right:
St Brendan. From an illuminated manuscript in the Bodleian Library.
below, right:
St Brendan and his monks at sea. From an illustrated manuscript in the Bodleian Library.

There are no authenticated portraits of Columbus. This one by an unknown artist, in the Gioviana Collection in the Civico Museo Archeologico, Como, best answers the physical description given by his son Ferdinand, and is thought by some scholars to be genuine.

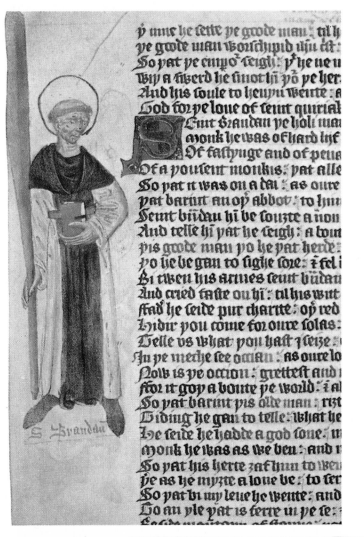

þ inne he sette þe gode man · til h[...]
þe gode man worschipid þn est ·
So þat þe empo[r] seigh · þ he ne [...]
Wiþ a swerd he smot hi vp þe her[...]
And his soule to heuyn wente · a[...]
God for þe loue of seint qurial[...]

S eint Brandan þe holi man [...]
monk he was of harde lif [...]
Of fastynge and of pen[...]
Of a þousent monkis · þat alle [...]
So þat it was on a dai · as oure [...]
þat barint an oþ abbot · to hi[...]
Seint bridau hi be souзte a non[...]
And telle hi þat he seigh · a þin[...]
þis gode man þo he þat herde ·
þo he be gan to siзhe sore · z fel i[...]
Bi twen his armes seint bridau[...]
And cried faste on hi · til his wit[...]
stad he seide pur charite · oþ red[...]
hidir þou come for oure solas ·
Telle vs what þou hast i seiзe · [...]
In þe meche see ocean · as oure lo[...]
Now is þe occion · grettest and [...]
for it goþ a boute þe world · z al[...]
So þat barint þis olde man · riзt[...]
Bidiug he gan to telle · what he [...]
he seide he hadde a god sone · m[...]
monk he was as we ben · and [...]
So þat his herte зaf him to wen[...]
he as he myзte a loue be · to ser[...]
So þat bi my leue he wente · and[...]
To an yle þat is ferre in þe se · [...]
[...]

Bartholomew de Las Casas, friend and biographer of Columbus, historian, and champion of the oppressed natives of the West Indies.

Granted that the earth was round it was clear that if a man sailed westward he must eventually reach the same point which Marco Polo had reached two centuries earlier by travelling eastward overland; and once the way had been pioneered the prospects both of profitable trade and of heathen souls to be saved were incalculable. No doubt Columbus discussed such things with his wife's family. In return, according to early biographers, da Cunha and young Perestrello passed on to him stories of a crudely-carved wooden idol that had been picked up at sea, of great canes capable of holding a gallon of wine between their joints which had been found on the beach at Porto Santo, of the trunks of strange trees and of the bodies of two men said to have been washed ashore on another island, 'very broad-faced and differing in every aspect from Christians'.

From Porto Santo Columbus and his family moved for a time to Funchal, Madeira, and here, so his biographers wrote, he received dramatic confirmation of his belief that inhabited land existed to the west. The story varies in detail, but emerges generally as follows.

One day a small, storm-wracked ship limped into Funchal, her crew of only five survivors in the last stages of hunger and exhaustion. Columbus took them into his home and did what he could to care for them, but they were beyond human aid and died one by one until only the ship's pilot, a Spaniard named Alonso Sanchez, of Huelva, remained.

The account Sanchez gave to Columbus before he too died was that he had sailed from Spain with a crew of seventeen on a trading voyage to England. When well out to sea the ship had encountered a fierce easterly gale which had driven it westward for twenty-eight days. Eventually Sanchez and his crew had seen some islands and had landed on one to obtain water and wood. Although Sanchez had tried to take bearings, and even drew a crude map for Columbus's benefit, he had no real idea where these islands lay, and his only positive information about them was that they were inhabited by natives who went naked.

The voyage homeward had been a long and arduous battle, often against adverse winds and mountainous seas. All notion of where they were had been lost, provisions had given out and before Madeira was reached thirteen of the crew had died from starvation and the sheer labour of keeping the ship afloat. Even the early biographers are divided on the possible truth of this story. Oviedo is sceptical and Las Casas has some reservations, but he states that it was generally known and accepted by Columbus's associates. If it were true the effect on Columbus must have been considerable.

In 1481 Columbus returned to Lisbon with his wife and infant son. In the same year King Alfonso V died and was succeeded by his son, John II, then aged twenty-five. Although Alfonso had exploited with some skill the discoveries made by Henry the Navigator's captains he had done comparatively little to extend further the geographical knowledge they had gained in their voyages. On the other hand John, although certainly not averse to profitable trade on the African coast, also had much of his great-uncle Henry's curiosity and perhaps even a touch of his genius and was quite as sure that a way to the Indies could be found by rounding Africa.

Soon after Columbus's return he entered the new king's service. In December 1481, as commander of a caravel, he set out to sail down the African coast with a fleet led by Admiral Diego d'Azambuja, and in the next few months he assisted in the building of a fort called São Jorge (St George) at Elmina on the Gold Coast. He seems to have done well, and returned to Lisbon in 1482 greatly enhanced in reputation and recognized as a first-class pilot and navigator.

In the same year there arrived in Lisbon a German named Martin Behaim, a man of formidable reputation, part genius and part charlatan, whose knowledge of navigation, geography and cartography was second to none. He was appointed adviser to a council which the king had created for the study and furtherance of navigation; in this capacity he compiled new tables of navigation far more accurate than any used before, introduced improvements in the rigging of ships, and devised improved navigational instruments, including a brass astrolabe to replace the wooden type hitherto used. In the ordinary course Columbus and Behaim would almost certainly have met and Behaim was a forward-thinking man. It is perhaps significant that soon after Behaim's arrival in Lisbon Columbus's idea of sailing across the Atlantic became transformed from a mere dream to a tangible proposition.

A MAN
OBSESSED

Felipa Columbus is thought to have died in 1483, probably soon after her husband's return from the Gold Coast. Columbus did not mention his wife in the many statements he made during the next nine years; and from this and the fact that about the time of her death Columbus approached King John to back him on a voyage across the Atlantic some historians have deduced that he was by now so obsessed with his great design that he felt little grief at her loss. This view seems uncharitable. Many men do their best to ignore grief by absorbing themselves more than ever in their work or whatever interests them most, and from what is known of Columbus's character this would seem far more likely.

His proposal to the king was straightforward. By a series of intricate calculations based on incorrect premises he had come to the conclusion that Japan and the outlying islands of China were a mere 750 leagues across the Atlantic. Perhaps he quoted the Florentine cosmographer Toscanelli, who believed that Japan was only about 200 miles beyond Antillia; and perhaps also the prophet Esdras, who had once stated that only a seventh of the globe was covered with water.

Whatever his authorities, all he asked were ships and men to enable him to make the voyage, and, of course, an adequate reward if he succeeded. Las Casas states that the conditions he laid down were that he should be appointed Supreme Admiral of the Ocean Sea and supreme governor, with the power of life and death, over any land he might discover, that he should receive a tenth of all revenue from these lands, and that he and his family in perpetuity should be granted a noble title.

There is some doubt whether he did in fact make such stipulations, but in any case it is highly unlikely King John would have approved them. On the other hand, John was clearly interested and impressed. However, instead of deciding the matter personally, which he could easily have done, he referred it to a council of his advisers comprising the Bishop of Ceuta, Dr José Vizinho and Dr Rodrigo, men of formidable academic ability and debating skill, equally versed in theology and all the sciences. When Columbus appeared before them he could find no answer to their learned arguments, and on their advice his proposal was rejected as impracticable and perhaps even heretical.

But the king and his council were far more interested than they were willing to admit. At the request of his interrogators Columbus drew a chart of his proposed route, and secretly, on the Bishop of Ceuta's advice, the king sent a caravel from the Cape Verde Islands to see whether there really was any land to the west. The expedition was a failure because the ship ran into such stormy weather that the crew became terrified and insisted that they return to port. However, the king was not deterred. In the following year, 1484, he licensed one Fernão Domingo de Arco, of Madeira, to search for an island in the west Atlantic; and two years later, with the support of Behaim, he authorized Fernão Dulmo, of the Azores, to make 'a distant voyage of discovery' to the west. Because a map produced by Behaim in 1492 showed land beyond the Atlantic it has been claimed that Dulmo

The island of Antillia is positively defined in this reproduction of a map of the Atlantic by Bartolomeo Pareto, dated 1455. British Museum.

The Gokestad right, and Oseberg below, ships, in the Ship Museum in Oslo, Norway. It was in such Ships as these that the first Norsemen voyaged from Greenland to the mainland of North America.

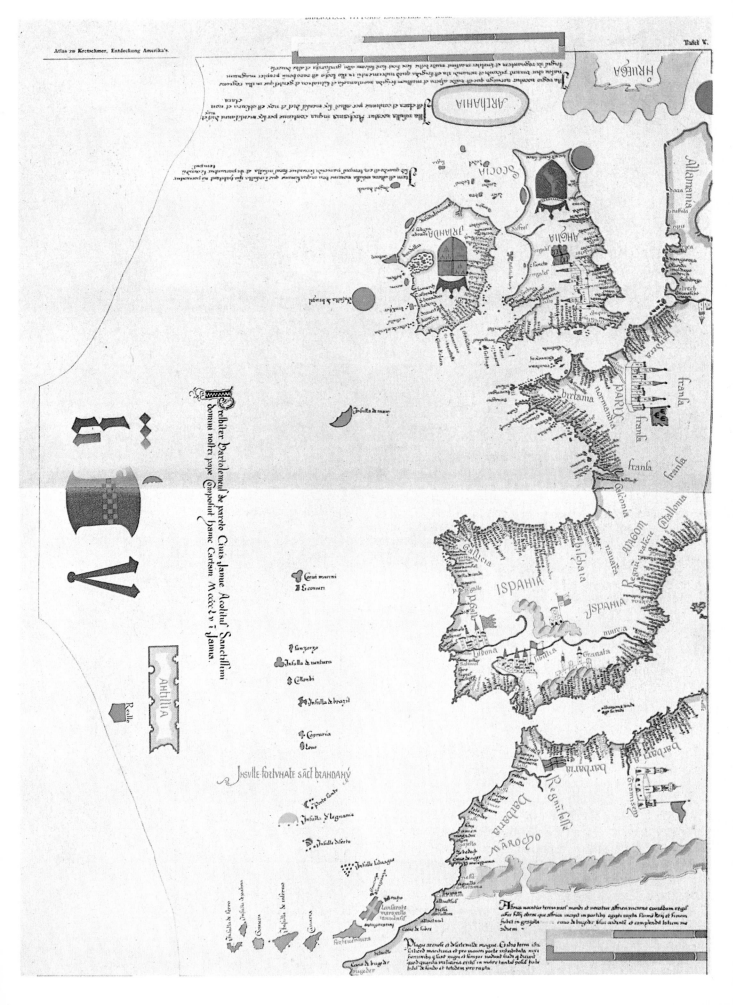

The hazards faced by voyagers in the fifteenth century are graphically if not very accurately portrayed in this engraving by Theodore de Bry.
above, right:
A sixteenth-century view of the city of Seville, which Columbus made his headquarters during much of his time in Spain.
right:
The Florentine cosmographer Paolo Toscanelli, whose geographical theories profoundly influenced Columbus. An existing letter suggests the two were in correspondence, but many scholars deny this and assert that the letter is a forgery.
far right:
King John II ('The Perfect') of Portugal.

did in fact find land, but if this is so the discovery was never made public and it seems more likely that Behaim's map was based on guesswork rather than knowledge.

By this time Columbus had left Portugal, taking his small son Diego. His departure was sudden and secret. Some say that he left in disgust when he learned of King John's treachery and others that he was forced to leave to escape his creditors. He entered Spain in the south at Huelva, and again there are two versions of what happened next. According to one, he left Diego in the care of his wife's sister Violante, who had married a man of Huelva named Muliantes; according to the other he left the boy with the Franciscan friars of La Rábida, a monastery outside the port of Palos. Now alone, Columbus continued on to the city of Seville, where for a time

he is thought to have become associated in business with some Genoese merchants there.

His shabby treatment in Lisbon had in no way discouraged Columbus. As enthusiastic as ever about his idea he discussed it freely with his new friends, and on their suggestion he decided to seek the powerful support of Don Luis de la Cerda, Count (and afterwards Duke) of Medina Celi, a man of considerable influence.

Medina Celi was warmly sympathetic and insisted that Columbus remain at Rota as his guest during the winter of 1485 so that they could discuss his plan in more detail. On the Count's own evidence he agreed to finance the voyage himself and to provide Columbus with 'three or four well-equipped caravels', but for reasons of diplomacy not without royal approval.

At this time Spain was a rapidly-growing power, united as never before under the joint rule of King Ferdinand and Queen Isabella. When they married in 1469 Isabella had been princess of Castile and Ferdinand prince and heir-apparent of Aragon, and for some time their influence was slight and their court modest. Their period of power began in 1474 when on the death of her brother Henry, Isabella had been proclaimed Queen of Castile and Léon, and it had been consolidated when Ferdinand succeeded to the crown of Aragon in 1479.

Isabella, born in the same year as Columbus, was a woman of rare qualities and gifts. Although brought up in seclusion her education had been far in advance of that of most women of her day. She was intelligent, generous, ambitious and a keen patron of learning and

far right:
The Genoa that Columbus knew in his youth.
Painting by Cristoforo Grassi, 1481. Museo Civico
Navale, Genoa.
far right, below:
The embarkation of the brothers Nicolo and Maffeo
Polo at Venice, with Nicolo's son Marco, in 1271.
Marco Polo, the greatest traveller of medieval
times, wrote an account of his travels which
largely inspired Columbus to seek a sea passage
to China by sailing westward from Europe.
From an illuminated MS in the Bodleian
Library, Oxford.
right:
The arrival of the Polos at Carcan on their historic
journey across Asia. From an illuminated MS in the
Bodleian Library, Oxford.
below:
The Polos presenting letters to the Grand Khan.
From an illuminated MS in the Bodleian Library,
Oxford.

the arts. Her moral influence over the Castilian court had been great, and she had raised it, as one historian wrote, 'from the debasement and degradation of her brother's reign to being a nursery of virtue'.

Ferdinand lacked her personality and charm, but he was a brilliant diplomat and took great pleasure in besting his rivals. Both were dedicated to the task of driving the Moors from their remaining strongholds in Spain, and both were ardent Catholics which meant, at that time, that they were also bigots. In 1480, without help from the Papacy, they had introduced their own version of the Inquisition to deal with heretics, and they were strongly anti-Semitic and determined to rid their country of Jews.

Wisely, Medina Celi approached Isabella rather than the king for approval of Columbus's proposal. Isabella was curious to know more about it, and may even at this stage have thought of the possibility of supporting it herself. Accordingly she ordered that Columbus be sent to the court which was then at Cordova. By the time he arrived on 20 January 1486, however, she and the king had left for Madrid, and he had to await her return.

In the interval he met Beatriz Enriquez de Harana, a daughter of peasants who had died during her childhood, and who now lived in Cordova with an uncle, a wine presser by trade. Beatriz, who was about twenty-one compared with Columbus's thirty-five, eventually became his mistress and in the summer of 1488 she bore him a son, Ferdinand. Marriage to a peasant's daughter would obviously have handicapped a man of Columbus's ambition; nevertheless it is clear that he remained very fond of her for the rest of his life, and in a codicil to his will he instructed his heir Diego to make sure that she was 'put in a way to live honourably, as a person to whom I am in great debt'.

The king and queen returned to Cordova after an absence of four months, and on 1 May 1486 Columbus had his first audience with Isabella. She received him graciously and listened with interest to his plan. Clearly it was too big a matter to be decided at a single interview, and to give herself time to think it over and discuss it with her advisers she arranged for her comptroller of finances, Alonso de Quintanilla, to look after Columbus and ordered that he be paid a small allowance. Quintanilla took Columbus into his home as a guest, and there he met on terms of social equality some of the most influential men in Spain. Columbus must have thought that most of his troubles were over. In fact they had barely begun.

Perhaps on her husband's advice the queen decided that Columbus's project should be examined by a committee of experts, which was headed by her confessor, Fray Hernando de Talavera, and included 'other wise and learned men and mariners'. The committee sat briefly at Cordova, and in the winter moved with the court to Salamanca, where its sittings were held in the university college of St Stephen.

After one unfortunate experience with committees Columbus was determined not to be humiliated again. To equip himself adequately to meet their scholarly arguments he sought the advice, as he wrote later, of 'learned men, priests and laymen, Latins and Greeks,

King Ferdinand of Spain. He was originally King of Aragon and Sicily. His marriage to Isabella began the unification of Spain.
Queen Isabella of Spain. She was a sovereign in her own right before her marriage to Ferdinand having inherited the crown of Castile and Leon. The patroness of Columbus, she was a gifted and resolute ruler. Spain's greatness was in large measure due to her.
right:
Moorish arches in the Great Mosque at Cordova. It was in the beautiful old city that Columbus enjoyed his first audience with Isabella. It was here also that he met Beatriz de Harana, who became his mistress and the mother of two of his sons.

Jews and Moors, and many others of other sects'. His spare hours were spent in intensive study, and he read 'all that has been written on geography, history, philosophy and other sciences'.

There is evidence, from surviving copies of books owned by Columbus and annotated in his hand and from other sources, that his reading included the works of Aristotle, the Greek geographer Strabo, the Egyptian astronomer and geographer Ptolemy, the *Imago Mundi* of Pierre d'Ailly, the *Historia Rerum Ubique Gestarum* of Pope Pius II, and a recent translation (1485) into Latin of *The Book of Ser Marco Polo*. His annotations in the d'Ailly work and the account of Polo's travels are particularly extensive and suggest that he relied largely on

far left:
Prince Henry of Portugal, known as Henry the Navigator. He was strongly influenced by Marco Polo's book, and inspired many of the great sea-faring achievements of the fifteenth century. Detail from the painting *St Vincent*, by Nuno Gonçalves.

left:
The Madonna of the Catholic Kings, a painting by an unknown artist in the Prado, Madrid. On one side can be seen Queen Isabella, and on the other King Ferdinand and their son Don Juan.

below:
Columbus and his son Diego at La Rábida. Painting by Delacroix.

these to bolster his arguments before the committee.

The tradition that Columbus's first task was to convince the committee that the world was a sphere may be safely discounted, for all but a few die-hard theologians already accepted this. His real task was to justify his claim that the Indies were within comparatively easy sailing distance westward. As his own calculations were so hopelessly wrong this was clearly impossible, and there is no evidence that his newly-acquired erudition made any impression on the committee. On the other hand they could hardly have failed to be impressed by his utter confidence in himself and his project. There is a familiar story that at one meeting Columbus produced an egg and challenged members of the committee to stand it on end. When they failed he simply flattened the end by breaking it so that the egg stood firmly erect, and then said in effect: 'You see, gentlemen, you can do anything when you know how.' Whether the story is true or not hardly matters. It is merely a reflection of Columbus's attitude, and its helps to explain why the committee did not reject his proposal summarily, as it might well have done.

In the long run their indecision was almost as hard to bear as outright rejection. As the months dragged on it became for Columbus, as Las Casas wrote, 'a terrible, continued, painful and prolonged battle'. The king and queen had become increasingly involved in the war against the Moors; and as it became apparent that Isabella's interest in Columbus and his scheme was waning, many at court who had once sought his company now scorned and openly insulted him. To make matters worse his allowance was discontinued, and in a state of utter pessimism he decided to turn again to Portugal.

During 1488 he wrote to King John II offering to return to Lisbon to reopen negotiations on condition that he was given a safe-conduct, probably against arrest by his creditors. The king's reply could hardly have been more encouraging. He called Columbus 'our particular friend', guaranteed him against detention for any reason, and begged him to come at once. The reason for this surprising warmth is not hard to find. None of the captains he had sent westward had ventured far enough to find land. In the summer of 1487 he had sent one of his best men, Bartholomew Diaz, with three ships to seek an eastern route to the Indies by way of the African coast and nothing had been heard of him in a year.

Had Columbus gone to Lisbon at once all might have been well. But instead he delayed, probably hoping for a decision from the Talavera committee, and the delay was disastrous. When he reached the Portuguese capital in December 1488 he was just in time to witness the triumphant return of Diaz. Far down the African coast his ships had been blown out to sea and when they turned north and came in sight of land again Diaz found that they had actually rounded the southern tip of the continent and were 200 miles beyond. On his way home he had stopped at what he, or perhaps the king in his elation, called *Cabo de Boa Esperança*, the Cape of Good Hope. In one of his book-annotations Columbus claims that he was actually at court when Diaz reported his success and gave John a chart of his voyage, 'plotted league by league'. Now that an eastward route to the Indies had been found Portugal obviously had no need of any other, and there is no record that Columbus's project ever reached the point of discussion.

The blow to Columbus must have been severe, but instead of losing heart he enlisted the aid of his brother Bartholomew, who was still in Lisbon. Bartholomew should seek royal backing in England and, if this failed, in France.

Bartholomew's movements from then on are shadowy. Although archival records are lacking in England both Ferdinand Columbus and Oviedo state definitely that he went to London and there eventually obtained an audience with Henry VII. England was still recovering economically from the War of the Roses, Henry was a parsimonious man, and England's days of seafaring greatness were still to come. Despite all this Ferdinand says the king was definitely interested, but Oviedo declares otherwise and says that the royal advisers treated the proposal as a joke and turned it down flatly.

Soon afterwards Bartholomew crossed to France. Although equally unsuccessful with the young King Charles VIII he won the sympathy and support of Charles's elder sister, Anne de Beaujeu, who was regent during his minority. Anne must have held out some hope of his eventual support for she persuaded Bartholomew to enter her service as a map-maker, and in fact he was still working at Fontainebleau in 1493 when word was received of Columbus's great success.

The Talavera commission could not have been pleased by Columbus's abortive attempt to reopen negotiations with King John. At the same time Spain could hardly afford to ignore Portugal's success. As she had found an eastward sea route to the Indies it was obviously in Spain's interest to find a westward route; and whatever the commission may have thought of the practicability of Columbus's proposal the fact remained that no one had yet come forward with a better one.

In spite of what Isabella must have regarded as Columbus's duplicity she still retained her faith in him and in his enterprise, but while Ferdinand remained pre-occupied with the war against the Moors, which was now approaching a favourable climax, there was little she could do. It was certainly no time for Columbus to press for a decision; his only course was to wait and hope.

Little is known for sure about where and how Columbus spent the next two years. It seems likely, however, that for much of the time he was in Cordova with his mistress Beatriz. According to one account she was now looking after young Diego as well as her infant son Ferdinand, and it is said that Columbus earned a precarious living at his old trade of book-selling. Certainly all communication with the court was not broken off. There is a record that in 1489, with the approval of Ferdinand and Isabella, he spent some time at the royal camp outside the besieged Moorish city of Baza, about fifty miles north-east of Granada, and he is said to have fought there as a volunteer with 'conspicuous valour'.

In the summer of 1490, when the court had moved to Seville, Columbus received what must have seemed to

him the final blow. After more than four years of desultory consideration the Talavera committee reported that it considered his proposal 'impossible and vain', and recommended its rejection. Apart from advancing various theological arguments that there could be nothing worth finding beyond the Atlantic, the committee was sure that the ocean was far wider than Columbus asserted. Even allowing it to be navigable, which was doubtful, it would take three years to reach Cathay, and there was no certainty that ships which undertook such a hazardous voyage would ever be able to return.

Ferdinand and Isabella were not unduly impressed. They neither rejected nor accepted this report, and sent word to Columbus, almost certainly on Isabella's insistence, that once the Moors were finally beaten they would be prepared to consider his proposal again.

But Columbus's patience was running out and in the summer of 1491 it was exhausted. Perhaps on a suggestion from Bartholomew or perhaps in sheer desperation he decided to go to France and offer his services to Charles VIII. In his absence Beatriz would, of course, look after Ferdinand. But some other arrangement would need to be made about Diego, who was now aged eleven, and Columbus may have decided to leave him again in the care of his sister-in-law at Huelva. The distance from Cordova to Huelva is 150 miles or more, and as Columbus could not afford to hire transport he and the boy had to walk. On the last stage of their long journey they passed through the port of Palos and at nightfall, tired and hungry, they stopped at the monastery of La Rábida and asked for bread and lodging.

Columbus could not have guessed how vitally this casual stop was to affect his future. He and Diego were welcomed inside, and the same evening Columbus told his story to Fray Juan Pérez, the head of the friary, who many years before had been confessor to the queen. Fray Juan was so interested that he called in Dr Garcia Fernandez, a local doctor who had studied astronomy and cosmography. Both agreed that the idea of reaching the Indies by sailing west was not only practicable but

from many points of view highly desirable.

Fray Juan persuaded Columbus to postpone his visit to France, and to stay on for a while at La Rábida. He then wrote to Isabella emphasizing his belief in Columbus's project and begging her to reopen the matter. By this time the royal couple were at Santa Fé from where Ferdinand was directing the siege of Granada, the last remaining stronghold of the Moors in Spain. Isabella's reply, received in about a fortnight, was favourable. She ordered Fray Juan to come to court and bade Columbus wait at La Rábida until he heard from her. That same night the friar left by mule. The arguments he submitted to Isabella were obviously impressive, and soon afterwards she wrote commanding that Columbus should appear at court and, having learned of his poverty, sent money for him to buy new clothes and to hire a mule.

At some time late in 1491 Columbus appeared once again at court and had another audience with the queen. She told him that she favoured his enterprise and would submit it for the approval of the Royal Council, but she made it clear that little could be done and certainly no final decision could be expected until after the fall of Granada. Yet again Columbus had to wait, but this time with more hope than ever before.

In addition to Fray Juan he soon gained other supporters, among them Luis de Santangel, who as keeper of Ferdinand's privy purse was a man of considerable influence at court, and Juan de Coloma, one of the king's most trusted advisers. Granada capitulated on 2 January 1492, and Columbus was among those who saw the defeated Moorish king hand over the keys of the stronghold to Ferdinand; later he took part in a triumphal march through the city.

Soon afterwards the royal council approved Columbus's scheme in principle, and it seemed as though, after six weary years, the battle was over. But with victory in his grasp Columbus announced, to the amazement of even his closest friends and supporters, that he would undertake the voyage only on certain terms. Basically they were the same as those which, according to Las Casas, he had demanded from John of Portugal, and in summary they amounted to the following:

(1) That Columbus and his heirs should have the title and office of Admiral in all the island and continents that he or they might discover.

(2) That he and his heirs should be viceroys and supreme governors over all such lands, with the right of nominating administrators of each island or province.

(3) That he and his heirs should be entitled, free of taxes, to a tenth of the net revenue from the products of all such lands.

(4) That he or a deputy appointed by him should have the right to adjudicate any case involving such products.

(5) That he and his heirs should have the right to contribute an eighth of the expenses of any expedition to the new lands and to receive an eighth of the profits.

The Royal Council was shocked and condemned these demands as exorbitant. Columbus's friends begged him to modify them but he would not. They were not, he

insisted, unreasonable. If he found nothing he would get
nothing. On the other hand, if he discovered new and
rich lands what he asked would be no more than a just
reward for his achievement. Inevitably the Council
recommended that the terms be refused; and the king
and queen, at what they made plain was a final audience,
informed Columbus that his project was finally and
absolutely rejected. The same day Columbus and Fray
Juan left by mule for La Rábida, the good friar no doubt
still bewildered by Columbus's apparent stubbornness.

It is hard to believe, however, that Columbus would
have nullified so recklessly the effort and heartache of
more than six years. He must surely have had some good
reason for what he did, and the most likely is that he
knew that pressure would be brought to bear on Ferdinand and Isabella to reverse their decision.

In fact this is precisely what happened. Almost before
Columbus was out of sight Luis de Santangel sought out
the queen, expressed his astonishment that she should
have turned down an enterprise involving 'so little risk,
yet which could prove of so great service to God and the
exaltation of His Church, not to speak of the very great
increase of glory for her realms and crown', and in case
money was the stumbling-block offered to finance the
expedition himself. Isabella was so completely won over
that she volunteered if need be to pawn her own jewels,
and at once sent word to recall Columbus. He was still
only four miles from Santa Fé when the messenger
arrived, and he and Fray Juan turned back at once.

Formal negotiations were reopened with Fray Juan
acting for Columbus, now from a position of strength,
and Juan de Coloma watching the royal interests. As such
negotiations are apt to be, they were protracted, even
though none of the issues were now really contentious.
On 17 April 1492 a document known as the Capitulation,
which granted all five demands made by Columbus, was
drawn up and signed by the royal couple. Next came the
Title, of 30 April, which stated that in the event of the
success of Columbus's mission he should be empowered
to entitle himself 'Don Cristóbal Colón, and his heirs and
successors for all time may be so entitled, and enjoy the
offices of Admiral of the Ocean Sea, Viceroy and Governor of the said islands and mainlands'.

On the same day Columbus received a royal passport,
three orders which had to do with the fitting out of the
three ships for the expedition, and several letters of
credence, one, so Las Casas declares, addressed to the
Grand Khan of China and the others left blank to be
filled in by Columbus according to whoever else of
importance he should meet.

Financial details were soon settled. The actual cost of
the expedition was small – a matter of 2,000,000 maravedis (in modern currency about £7,000) with in addition
a monthly payroll of 250,000 maravedis. The royal
treasury contributed about two-thirds of the total,
Columbus himself invested 250,000 maravedis which he
must have borrowed, the rest was found by Santangel.

The problem of providing ships was solved neatly and
economically. Ferdinand and Isabella issued a royal
decree informing the people of Palos that 'for certain
things done and committed by you to our disservice, you

A general view of Granada. The capture of the
Moorish capital occupied the attention of
Ferdinand and Isabella to the exclusion of all else –
its surrender would mean the Catholic monarchy's
undisputed supremacy in Spain. Columbus waited
on this event, and was actually present at the
surrender on 2 January 1492.

A page of the Capitulation of Santa Fé, in which
the Spanish sovereigns agreed to Columbus's
terms for his first voyage.

are condemned and obligated by our Council to provide us for a twelvemonth with two equipped caravels at your own proper charge and expense', and Columbus was authorized to charter a third, which was to be his flagship. The ship he chartered was the *Santa Maria*, those provided by the people of Palos were the *Pinta* and *Niña*.

The *Santa Maria* was a three-masted ship of about 100 tons or a little more, with high superstructures fore and aft called 'castles', of a total length of about ninety feet and a beam of twenty feet. Columbus was proud of her at first, but soon found her 'a dull sailer and unfit for discovery'. The *Pinta* was perhaps of sixty tons and the *Niña* slightly less. Both were of shallow draught which enabled them to sail close to land, and fairly fast sailers.

Columbus himself commanded the *Santa Maria*, his master was the ship's owner Juan de la Cosa (not to be confused with the famous cartographer of the same period), and among his company of about forty was Luis de Torres, a converted Jew, who was taken along hopefully as an interpreter because he spoke Hebrew and some Arabic. The *Pinta* was commanded by Martin Alonso Pinzón, a noted ship-owner and pilot of Palos, and the *Niña* by his brother Vicente. The *Pinta's* complement was about twenty-six and the *Niña's* about two less. There was a total of about ninety seamen.

In case Columbus had any trouble in enlisting crews for such a venturesome voyage royal pardons were offered to any prisoners under sentence who volunteered, but few took advantage of the offer and most of those who sailed were experienced seamen of Palos. Each ship carried a doctor, but surprisingly, in view of the devoutness of the royal couple and Columbus himself, there were no priests. Nor were there any men-at-arms or marines. However, suits of light armour and protective helmets known as *morions* were carried with an armoury of swords, pikes, crossbows and *espingardas* (the primitive muskets of the day), and each ship was equipped with small cannon called *lombards*. Each ship was provisioned for a year but Columbus was confident he would be back much sooner than that.

Las cosas suplicadas e que vuestras Altezas dan e otorga a don xpoual de
Colon en alguna satisfaçion delo que ha descubierto enlas mares
oceanas y del viaje q agora conel ayuda de dios ha de fazer por
ellas enseruiçio de vuestras altezas son las q siguen

Primeramente que vuestras al. como Señores que son delas dichas mares oceanas fazen dende
agora al dicho don xpoual y Colon su almirante en todas aquellas yslas y tierras fir
mes q porsu mano o Industria se descubriere o ganare enlas dichas mares oceanas
para durante su vida y despues del muerto asus herederos e suçessores epetuamente
peteneçientes al tal offiçio e segund q don alfonso enrriquez q al mirante mayor
de castilla e los otros sus predeçessores enel dicho offiçio lo tenian en sus distritos
Plaze asus altezas. Johan de coloma

Otrosi que vuestras al. fazen al dicho don xpoual su visorrey e gouernador gnal en todas
las dichas tierras firmes e yslas que como dicho es el descubriere o ganare enlas
dichas mares e que parel regimiento de cada vna eqalquiere dellas faga el elecçio
de tres personas pa cada offiçio e que vuestras al. tomen y escojan vno el que mas fuere
su seruiçio e asi seran mejor regidas las tierras q nro señor le dexara fallar e
ganar aseruiçio de vuestras al. Plaze asus altezas. Johan de coloma

Item q de todas eqalesquiere mercadurias siquiere sean plas piedras preçiosas
oro plata speçeria e otras qualesquiere cosas e mercadurias de qualquiere speçie
nobre e maña q sean q se comprare trocare fallare ganare e ouiere dentro en
los limytes del dicho almirantadgo q dende agora vuestras altezas fazen merçed
al dicho don xpoual e quiere q haya e lleue para si la dezena parte de todo
ello quitadas las costas todas q se fiziere en ello por maña q delo q quedare
limpio e libre haya e tome la dicha dezena parte pa si mismo e faga dello
asu voluntad quedando las otras nueue partes para vuestras altezas Plaze asus
altezas Johan de coloma

Otrosi que si acausa delas mercadurias quel traera delas dichas yslas y tierras
q asi como dicho es se ganaren o descubriere o delas q entruequo de aquellas se
tomaran aqua de otros mercaderes naçere pleyto alguno enel logar dond el dicho
comerçio e trato se terna y fara q si por el preheminençia de su offiçio de almi
rante le peteneçera conoçer del tal pleyto plega a vuestras altezas q el o su te
niente e no otro Juez conozcan del tal pleyto e asi lo prouean dende agora
Plaze asus altezas si perteneçe al dicho offiçio de almirante segund q lo tenyo
el dicho almirante don alonso enrriquez e los otros sus anteçessores en sus dis
tritos y siendo justo. Johan de coloma

Item q en todos los nauios q se armare parael dicho trato e negoçiaçion cada y quando
y quantas vezes se armare que pueda el dicho don xpoual colon si quisiere
contribuyr e pagar la ochena parte de todo lo q se gastare enel armazo
e q tanbien haya e lleue del prouecho la ochena parte delo q resultare
dela tal armada Plaze asus altezas. Johan de coloma

Son otorgadas e despachadas conlas respuestas de vuestras altezas en fin
de cada vno Capitulo enla villa de Santa fe de la vega de granada

THE FIRST VOYAGE

All was ready by 2 August 1492. Early next morning, a Friday, Columbus and his officers and men received communion in the little church of St George at Palos. Before sunrise anchors had been weighed, and by eight a.m. the three ships had crossed the river bar and were heading south.

Columbus's plan was simple. Although he had no means of assessing longitude except by dead reckoning he would be able in calm weather to calculate his approximate latitude with the aid of either an astrolabe or an astronomical quadrant. He knew that the Canary Islands and Japan were in about the same latitude, so he proposed to go first to the Canaries and then to sail more or less due west, on the assumption that even if he missed Japan he must eventually reach the coast of China.

The account of the voyage comes from Columbus's own journal. The original has long since disappeared, but Las Casas had access to it, and from it he produced an abridged version. This is a curious document which sometimes uses Columbus's own words and is in the first person and sometimes paraphrases the journal and speaks of Columbus in the third person as 'the Admiral'. It omits nautical details, it is often inaccurate, and it includes much interpolated by Las Casas himself. Despite its faults, however, it is an invaluable record of what is generally agreed to have been the most important single voyage in history.

On 6 August, three days out from Palos, the fleet suffered its first mishap when the rudder of the *Pinta* jumped its gudgeons. This has been claimed as a deli-berate act of sabotage by the caravel's owner, Cristóbal Quintero, or by some of her crew who had already lost their enthusiasm for a long voyage in strange and danger-ous seas, but the evidence is inconclusive. While the damage was being repaired at Gomera, one of the main islands of the Canaries, wood, water and fresh provisions were taken aboard all three ships, and the *Niña's* lateen rig was altered to square, 'that she might follow the other vessels with more tranquility and less danger'.

On 6 September the fleet sailed from San Sebastian, the port of Gomera, and after a couple of days of adverse winds the voyage into the unknown began in earnest. From the start Columbus deliberately understated the daily distance sailed, or, as Las Casas wrote, 'counted less than the true number of leagues, so that the crew would not be dismayed or frightened should the voyage prove long', and presumably his other captains were ordered to do the same. Thus, for example, on 10 September Columbus calculated that the ships had sailed sixty leagues but told his crew that they had covered only forty-eight; and next day the figures were forty and thirty-two respectively.

For days on end the sea was calm, the wind blew steadily and favourably and the weather was delightful, 'like that of Andalusia in April', Columbus wrote. On 16 September, ten days out from Gomera, large patches of 'very green grass' were seen and it was thought they must be near some island. In fact the 'grass' was seaweed and they were entering the Sargasso Sea, which stretches from about longitude 32° west almost to the Bahamas. In

little more than a week the fleet had covered more than 1,000 miles, mostly with the *Santa Maria* bringing up the rear and with the *Pinta*, the fastest sailer of the three, well ahead and forced every now and then to take in sail to allow the others to catch up.

Despite the almost ideal conditions the very steadiness of the trade wind was already troubling the seamen, who wondered how they would be able to sail back to Spain against it; and they became so restless that Columbus was almost relieved when, on 20 September, he ran out of the trade belt and was obliged to change course to west by north. Variable winds were followed by calms and light airs, and again the seamen became alarmed. With no wind at all, they complained, it would be equally impossible for them to return home.

About sunset on 25 September Martin Alonso Pinzón shouted excitedly from the poop of the *Pinta* that he could see land and claimed the reward of an annuity of 10,000 maravedis which the king and queen had promised to the first man to do so. On all three ships men climbed into the rigging and it was generally agreed that land was in sight about twenty-five leagues to the south-west. Columbus knelt and offered thanks to God, all hands sang *Gloria in excelsis Deo*, and course was altered towards the supposed land.

Although the ships sailed about eighty miles during the night dawn brought no sign of land, and Columbus recorded disappointedly that what had been seen was 'merely cloud'. Twelve days later the *Niña*, which was out in front, hoisted a flag and fired a gun to signal that she had sighted land, but again there was none.

This second disappointment was too much. By 10 October, Las Casas wrote, 'the men could suffer it no longer'. Their discontent and fear had spread to the officers, and there were dark threats of mutiny and of throwing Columbus overboard if he refused to turn back. But Columbus's faith in himself and his enterprise remained firm. He tried at first to win them over by reminding them of the great wealth they would gain and the honours they would receive on their return to Spain, and when this failed he told them flatly that 'their complaints were to no purpose, for he was determined to find the Indies and meant to continue on until with God's help he did so'. Finally, according to Oviedo's account, a compromise was reached and Columbus agreed that if no land was sighted within three days he would turn for home.

Next day the signs were propitious. The *Niña* picked up a green branch with flowers on it and the *Pinta* retrieved a piece of cane, a pole, a small carved stick and a land plant. Land birds flew overhead and there was a scent of land in the air. About ten o'clock that night Columbus saw ahead what seemed to him 'like the light of a small wax candle moving up and down'. His officers strained their eyes but could see nothing. Soon after-

Columbus's departure from Palos. Although shown in the picture, Ferdinand and Isabella were not actually there to say farewell to him. Engraving by Theodore de Bry.

Models of the *Santa Maria* and *Pinta* by Augustus
F. Crabtree, in the Mariners' Museum, Newport
News, Virginia.

De Bry's allegorical engraving, *The Vision of Columbus.*
right:
Page of a passport issued by Ferdinand and Isabella to Columbus, possibly for use on his first voyage.

wards Rodrigo de Triana, a seaman on the *Pinta*, reported land ahead, and by two a.m. it was visible to all at a distance of about six miles. Sails were shortened and the ships stood off-and-on for the rest of the night.

Daylight revealed that they were off the lee shore of an island about twelve miles long, and rather than risk what could be a dangerous landing Columbus took his ships round to its western side where a bay was found which offered what appeared a safe anchorage. Naked Indians appeared and watched while Columbus and his officers were rowed ashore. Columbus carried a royal standard and the Pinzón brothers each a banner of the expedition, on which was a green cross with the initials of their sovereigns embroidered on them with a crown over each.

As he stepped on to the beach Columbus dropped to his knees, gave thanks to God and wept for joy. The royal standard was planted and 'with appropriate ceremony' Columbus named the island San Salvador and formally claimed it for his Sovereigns. Scholars seeking to identify the island still argue among themselves, but it is usually accepted that San Salvador is identical with Watling's Island, one of the Bahamas, and that the landing was made on the shore of Fernandez or Long Bay.

A great crowd of Indians, mostly young men, watched but made no attempt to interrupt the ceremony. They seemed so friendly that Columbus decided that they could 'more easily be converted to our Holy Faith by love than by force', and as a first token of his affection he distributed among them some red caps, glass beads and other trifles. Later some swam out to the ships with parrots, balls of cotton thread, spears and other articles and bartered these for beads and hawks' bells, the tinkling of which delighted them greatly.

The Indians' own name for their island, Columbus learned, was Guanahaní. His charts showed him an archipelago to the north of Japan, and he had no doubt it was one of these, and that within easy reach lay Japan itself, where the emperor's palace, according to Marco Polo, was roofed with gold and pearls.

The natives of Guanahaní seemed to Columbus 'a very poor people in everything'. Physically they were admirable – tall, well-made and handsome, with broad foreheads, large eyes and straight, black hair, like a horse's mane. They appeared to have no iron, and the only weapons he saw were spears, some sharpened to a fine point and some pointed with fishes' teeth. At sea they travelled swiftly in dugout canoes, some big enough to hold forty-five men, 'wonderfully made all in one piece from the bole of a tree'. They seemed a quiet, gentle and intelligent people, and he thought they would be 'good servants and of good skill'.

Apparently they had no religion and assumed that the white strangers had come down from the sky, and it would be easy, he felt, to make Christians of them. In fact the natives of Guanahaní and all the others whom Columbus met on this voyage were Tainos, descendants of a language group known as Arawaks who had migrated from the South American mainland and, after conquering the primitive aborigines, had settled in the Bahamas, Cuba, Jamaica and Haiti. As Columbus was to learn they were by no means as poor as he thought from his first contact with them. They lived in well-made palm-thatched huts, cultivated corn, sweet potatoes and other root vegetables, made a sort of bread from cassava or yucca root, spun and wove cotton, and made pottery.

As they spoke neither Hebrew nor Arabic, Columbus's interpreter was of little use, and all communication had to be by signs. Columbus's main quest was for gold, and as some of the ornaments the Indians wore were of this metal he questioned them closely about where it had been obtained. They pointed to the south – where he believed Japan to lie – and he gathered from their signs that there he would find a king who possessed 'great vessels of gold and huge quantities of it'. However, they declined his request to guide him to the place. On a boat tour of the island Columbus saw two or three villages, the natives of which welcomed him warmly and swam out with water and food. He noted a spot where a fort could be built. 'With fifty men', he wrote, 'I could conquer the

Martin Alonso Pinzón, captain of the *Pinta* on Columbus's first voyage.

whole island and govern it as I pleased.'

The ships stayed two days, and when they sailed southward on the evening of 14 October they had on board seven natives whom Columbus had detained to act as guides and interpreters, and whom he planned to take back to Spain. Next day another island was seen which Columbus named Santa Maria de la Concepción and which appears on modern maps as Rum Cay. Here one of the captives from Guanahaní leapt overboard from the *Niña* and escaped with the aid of the local natives.

Another local native who had come alongside in his canoe to trade was seized to replace the absconder, but on Columbus's orders he was treated kindly, given some presents – 'worth not more than four maravedis', Columbus noted – and released. Again Columbus inquired about gold, and again he was told that there was plenty of it to the south, where the Indians wore bracelets of gold on their arms and legs. Among presents brought to the ship were some dried leaves which the natives seemed to value highly and which were undoubtedly

A clerk's copy of a ration list drawn up for Columbus.
above, right:
De Bry's impression of the landing at San Salvador, with natives offering gold and other gifts.
right:
The cipher of Columbus which always accompanied his signature. Scholars still argue as to its meaning.

the native island tobacco.

Among other islands which Columbus discovered, named and explored during the next week were Fernandina (Long Island), Isabella (Crooked Island), and a string of tiny cays forming part of the Bahama Bank which he called Islas de Arena. He was enchanted by everything he saw, and his journal became rhapsodical. The islands, he wrote, were 'the best, the most fertile, temperate and beautiful' in the world. Flocks of brilliantly-hued parrots darkened the sky; the melody of the birds was 'exquisite', and there were so many kinds of them, so different from those in Spain, that it was 'a marvel'. He had never seen trees and plants so green and so beautiful, and the scent of their flowers was 'the sweetest thing in the world'. Of trees alone, he thought, there must be a thousand kinds, each with its own fruit, and he was 'the saddest man in the world to be unable to recognise them, for I am sure they are all valuable'. On the other hand there seemed to be a complete lack of animals, though plenty of reptiles including some

huge lizards, probably iguanas, were seen.

Again and again the natives told him that if he wanted gold he must sail south. They spoke repeatedly of two much larger islands which they called Colba (Cuba) and Bofio (Haiti), where, they said, there were many ships and great sailors. Their descriptions of Cuba and its size confirmed his own belief that it must be Japan, and he decided that his next call would be there. Nevertheless, he wrote, he was still determined to continue on to the mainland of China, so that he could visit the city of Quinsay and present his letters of credence to the Great Khan. He reached the north coast of Cuba on 28 October and anchored in the harbour of a river 'very beautiful and with no danger of shoals' which Columbus called San Salvador. Scholars still argue as to its exact location, but the most favoured one is Bahia Bariay, near the present town of Antilla. It was a spot of ravishing beauty, of flowering and fruit-bearing trees and of little birds 'which sang very sweetly'. But the only people seen were naked Indian fishermen who fled when they saw

the ships, and Columbus looked in vain for any sign of Oriental civilization.

Next day he sailed westward, where his captive guides assured him he would find a city with a king, but all he found were some native villages which the inhabitants deserted on the approach of his men. In the villages were found many wooden statues in the shape of women and heads carved like masks, some domestic dogs that grunted instead of barking, some tamed birds and a great deal of fishing gear.

Adverse winds obliged the ships to double back on their tracks, and for some days they clung to the coast still looking for the elusive city. The Indians soon got over their fear of the strangers and came out in canoes with spun cotton and other goods to trade, but Columbus declined to accept these and let it be known that all he sought was *nucay*, which was their name for gold.

By now Columbus had decided that this was not Japan but the mainland of China. When local natives indicated that there was a large town inland ruled by a

A woodcut of 1494. The arrival of Columbus in the New World is rather fancifully depicted here, two years after the event. European houses stand on islands where no European had ever set foot.

powerful cacique or chief he assumed this must be Marco Polo's Zaitun or Quinsay and that the chief must be the Grand Khan himself, so he decided to send an embassy there comprising Rodrigo de Jérez and the interpreter, Luis de Torres, with two natives as guides. While they were away Columbus improved his acquaintance with the local Indians, including some old men who assured him that farther east on the island of Bofio there was gold 'in infinite quantity' and also pearls, and obligingly confirmed stories by the fictitious traveller, Sir John Mandeville, of one-eyed men and others with the heads of dogs, who beheaded their prisoners, drank their blood and then ate them.

On their trek inland the embassy met many people, and noted that men and women carried a firebrand and herbs to smoke which, according to the later account by Las Casas, 'gave a soothing effect and almost intoxication and relieved them from weariness'. For smoking, these herbs were rolled into tubes which were called *tobacos*. The supposed city turned out to be a village of about fifty huts with a few hundred inhabitants and the cacique was just another Indian. The visitors were well received and pressed to stay for a week or so, but they remained only one day. Their report disappointed Columbus, but did not shake his conviction that he was in China.

After being held up for four days by headwinds the ships resumed their voyage east on 12 November. With them they took, more or less by forcible abduction, six men, seven women and three boys. Columbus told these people that if he found gold he would set them free, but his real intention was to take them to Spain. Two of the men escaped a few days later. Some time was spent in vain search for an island which the natives called Babeque, and where, they said, the inhabitants gathered gold on the beach by candlelight and beat it into bars.

On 21 November Martin Alonso Pinzón left the other ships and continued eastward in the *Pinta*, 'without permission and against the wishes of the Admiral', so Las Casas wrote, 'and driven only by his greed for gold'. Columbus accepted this mutinous act with remarkable tolerance and merely noted that Pinzón had caused him 'many other troubles by word and deed'.

Soon afterwards the *Santa Maria* and *Niña* sailed beyond the eastern extremity of Cuba and Columbus was forced to admit that it could not be China after all. During 5 December the ships crossed the Windward Passage which separates Cuba from Haiti, and next day they entered a safe and extensive harbour on the northwest tip of Haiti which Columbus called Puerto de San Nicolas, a name it retains to this day. He was deeply impressed by the beauty of the port, but as the natives fled at his approach he saw no point in lingering.

Next morning the ships were on their way again coasting eastward, and in the afternoon they anchored in another harbour which Columbus called Puerto de la Concepción but which his seamen renamed, less romantically, but with much more accuracy Mosquito Bay. A few miles offshore was an island about twenty miles long which, from its general likeness to a tortoise, Columbus called Isla de la Tortuga and which in a later age was to become notorious as a haunt of pirates.

On 12 December Columbus caused a great cross to be raised on the shore of Mosquito Bay, took formal possession of the new land he had discovered for Ferdinand and Isabella, and called it Española, or, as it was to become known in its Latinized version, Hispaniola. This time Columbus did not make the mistake of believing himself to be in China but accepted the word of the Indians aboard that Hispaniola was a large island and that beyond it lay a mainland called Caribata, whose inhabitants were slave-raiders and cannibals.

The day the cross was raised three seamen captured 'a young and very beautiful girl', naked except for a piece of gold in her nose. After her fears had been allayed by the Indians aboard the ships she was inclined to stay, but Columbus ordered her to be put ashore in the hope that she would report favourably to her people of the white strangers. Next day he sent nine men ashore with an Indian interpreter. They followed a track inland to a village of about a thousand huts, the inhabitants of which fled at their approach.

above, left:
This curiously-shaped wooden idol is an interesting example of the carving of the Arawak-speaking Indians of the Greater Antilles. It is possibly from Cuba or Hispaniola.
left:
Three small stone ceremonial figures from the West Indies. The centre one represents an Indian god, and those on left and right are *celts*, instruments resembling chisels.

An elaborately carved pestle of the West Indies.
top, left:
A stone axe of the West Indies.
above, left:
A crudely carved wooden *zemi*, an idol or deity endowed with magic power. Columbus and his men found one or more of these in almost every hut they entered in Hispaniola.

However, they soon regained their courage and crowded around the newcomers, offering them cassava bread and fish, and presenting them with tame parrots. The Indians, they told Columbus on their return to the ships, were handsomer than those of Cuba and two girls they had seen were 'as white as those in Spain'. The land was beautiful and fertile, 'a terrestial Paradise', and the birds sang like nightingales. But they had found no gold.

The ships sailed again on 15 December, and after beating against headwinds for some days they got through Tortuga Channel and anchored beyond off a beach. The news had spread that the white men meant no harm and they were welcomed by about 500 Indians, among them a chief aged about twenty-one who was borne by four men on a sort of litter. Columbus sent a gift ashore to him, and the same evening the young chief came aboard the *Santa Maria*. He was received with 'due honour' and offered Spanish food, which he accepted politely and, after taking a single mouthful, passed on to his retainers. Columbus was delighted to note that many of the Indians wore gold ornaments, and a few articles were obtained next day by barter. The gold, he was assured, was not found locally, but – as he interpreted their signs to mean – in some islands about 100 leagues away where it was collected by the inhabitants, sifted, smelted and made into bars and 'a thousand wrought articles'. One of these islands, they declared, was entirely made of gold. 'Our Lord in his piety guide me that I may find it,' Columbus wrote fervently in his journal.

Relations with the natives continued friendly as the ships moved farther east. Expeditions were sent into the country, Columbus received a handsome present from the cacique Guacanagarí, who ruled the whole of north-western Haiti, and on occasions upwards of 1,500 Indians paddled or swam out to the ships bringing gifts and articles to barter. Farther east, Columbus was told, was an area which they called Cibao where there was 'a very great quantity of gold', and he easily persuaded himself this must be Cipangu, which was Marco Polo's name for Japan.

far left:
Columbus propounding his theory of a New World to Fray Pérez at La Rábida.
left:
The inn at Cordova where Columbus stayed at the time he met Beatriz de Harana. Painting by Joaquin Sorolla y Bastida.
below:
The Hall of the Kings and the Court of Lions in the Alhambra, Granada. After the triumph of Ferdinand and Isabella over the Moors the beautiful fortress-palace was allowed to decay. Restoration was not undertaken until the nineteenth century.

Farther east on the coast of Hispaniola, however, he had obtained a considerable quantity by barter, including nuggets 'as big as two fingers and some as big as a fist', and this he had divided equally between himself and his crew. There is a story also, which does not appear in Columbus's journal, that Pinzón had gone inland and met a powerful cacique named Caonabó who had given him a great deal of gold, and this may have been true, for the district Caonabó ruled was Cibao, which was then and still is the island's main gold-producing area.

With two ships again Columbus now had the choice of staying to explore further and to pursue his search for gold or of sailing directly for Spain. He decided on the latter for two main reasons. Admittedly he had failed to find China and Japan but he still believed he was within easy reach of them, and in any case even though his holds were not overflowing with treasure there could be no doubt that he had made some momentous discoveries and his natural wish was to report his achievement to Ferdinand and Isabella as soon as possible.

The second reason was that he still distrusted Pinzón and his clique, and feared that if they stayed longer there would be further trouble, whereas once back in Spain he would 'no longer have to endure the behaviour of evil men who behave contrary to the orders of him who has so honoured them'.

For another week the ships sailed leisurely eastward. On 13 January they made their final anchorage at a spot which Columbus called Bahia de las Flechas, Bay of the Arrows, because here for the first time he found unfriendly natives armed with bows and arrows and prepared to use them on the slightest provocation. Rather than risk an armed clash Columbus abandoned a tentative plan to careen and recaulk the ships, both of which were leaking badly, and on 16 January with a favourable wind they put to sea 'turning their prows east and by north'.

For a while it seemed that Columbus would be as fortunate on the homeward run as on the outward. A westerly trade wind blew, the ships were logging

The fort at La Navidad under construction.
above, right:
The cacique Guacanagari pays a ceremonial visit to
Columbus at the fort of La Navidad.
left:
Indian method of wine-making. From a sixteenth-
century history of the New World.

well over 100 miles a day and even up to 135, the air was
'very soft and sweet as in Seville during the spring', and
the sea, 'thanks be to God was always very smooth'.

On 13 February the weather changed for the worse.
'During the night the wind increased and the seas were
appalling', Las Casas wrote, paraphrasing Columbus,
'and the huge waves met one another so that the ship
could not escape as they broke over her.' There was no
choice but to run before the storm under bare poles and
hope for the best. Although flare signals were exchanged
the two ships lost touch and by dawn the *Pinta* was out
of sight. Daybreak brought no relief. Tremendous cross-
seas continued to sweep the *Niña's* deck, she rolled
alarmingly for lack of ballast in her holds, and the wind
rose steadily to near-hurricane force. Columbus and
everyone else on board prayed fervently, convinced their
last hour had come, and every man vowed that if the ship
were saved they would make a devout pilgrimage 'in
procession in their shirts' to the first shrine of the Virgin
they encountered.

During that day the storm abated slightly, and next
morning, 15 February, land was seen ahead. Then, however, the wind shifted suddenly and three more days
passed before anchor was thankfully dropped in a reason-
ably sheltered bay in what proved to be the Portuguese
island of Santa Maria, the most southerly and one of the
smallest of the Azores.

Here there was to be trouble of a different kind. Not
far from the anchorage, Columbus learned, there was a
small chapel dedicated to Our Lady, and remembering
the vow they had all made he sent half his crew ashore
clad only in their shirts to offer thanks for having been
saved. The astounded Portuguese watched them come
ashore and crowd into the tiny building. Then, as they
were on their knees in prayer, 'the whole town, on horse
and afoot, fell upon them and took them prisoners'. Later
an armed party came out to the caravel but Columbus
angrily refused to allow them aboard and threatened to
conquer the island by force.

The stalemate continued for some days until the local

53

left:
The departure of Columbus from Palos. Painting on a marble-topped table in the Mariners' Museum, Newport News, Virginia.
below, left:
Among other things Queen Isabella of Spain was noted for her patronage of the arts. Her large collection included this superb version of *The Temptation of Christ*, by Juan de Flandes.
below:
The mosaic in the Palazzo Tussi, Genoa, by Antonio Salviati. It is known as a portrait of Columbus — but compare this with the frontispiece portrait by an unknown artist.

¶ Epistola Christofori Colom: cui etas nostra multum debet: de Insulis Indie supra Gangem nuper inuentis Ad quas perqueren/ das octauo antea mense auspiciis z ere inuictissimoz Fernãdi z Helisabet Hispaniaz Regu missus fuerat: ad magnificum dñm Gabrielem Sanchis eozundem serenissimoz Regum Tesaurariũ missa: quã nobilis ac litteratus vir Leander de Cosco ab Hispa no idiomate in latinum conuertit tertio kals Maii· M·cccc·rciii· Pontificatus Alexandri Serti Anno primo·

Quoniam suscepte prouintie rem perfectam me psecutum fuisse gratum tibi fore scio: has constitui exarare: que te vniuscuiusq rei in hoc nostro itinere geste inuenteq ad/ moneant: Tricesimotertio die postq Gadibus discessi in mare Indicũ perueni: vbi plurimas insulas innumeris habitatas ho minibus repperi: quarum omnium pro feliciffimo Rege nostro preconio celebrato z verillis ertensis contradicente nemine pos sessionem accepi: primeq earum diui Saluatozis nomen impo/ sui: cuius fretus aurilio tam ad hanc: q ad ceteras alias perue/ nimus·Eam vo Indi Guanabanin vocant·Aliarũ etiam vnam quãq nouo nomine nuncupaui: quippe aliã insulam Sancte Marie Conceptionis· aliam Fernandinam· aliam Hysabellam· aliam Joanam· z sic de reliquis appellari iussi·Cum primum in eam insulam quam dudum Joanam vocari diri appulimus: iu rta eius littus occidentem versus aliquantulum procesfi: tamq eam magnam nullo reperto fine inueni: vt non insulã: sed conti nentem Chatai prouinciam esse crediderim: nulla tñ videns op pida municipiaue in maritimis sita confinib preter aliquos vi cos z predia rustica: cum quoz incolis loqui nequibam· quare si mul ac nos videbant surripiebant fugam· Progrediebar vltra: existimans aliquã me vrbem villasue inuenturũ· Deniq videns q longe admodum progressis nihil noui emergebat: z huiõi via nos ad Septentrionem deferebat: q ipse fugere exoptabã: terris etenim regnabat bzuma: ad Austrumq erat in voto cõtendere:

On the island of Santa Maria on his way home from the first voyage Columbus wrote a long account of his achievement to Luis de Santangel, one of his friends at court. This was published in a number of editions in various languages and quickly became a best-seller. Picture shows the first page of the Latin edition.

Woodcut from a 1493 edition in Latin of Columbus's letter to Luis Santangel.
right:
The Plaza del Rey, Barcelona, where Columbus was received by Ferdinand and Isabella on his return from his first voyage.

priest, acting as an intermediary, was able to study Columbus's papers and convince the garrison captain that his apparently fantastic story of being an Admiral of Spain and of having come from 'the Indies' was in fact true. The prisoners were then released and Columbus was allowed to take on water and a little fresh food.

The *Niña* left Santa Maria on 24 February. She was now in known waters and Columbus was justified in hoping that his troubles were over. Two days out she ran into another storm quite as severe as the first, and for a terrifying week she was battered in mountainous cross-seas and tossed about by winds so furious that she seemed to be 'carried up to the skies'. Again there were fears that she would founder at any moment; again mass prayers were offered up for deliverance. Even Columbus was desperately afraid and said so in his journal.

At daybreak on 4 March land was in sight. Columbus recognized it as the Rock of Sintra near the entrance to the River Tagus on which Lisbon stands. Columbus had no wish to risk arrest by landing on Portuguese territory,

but the storm continued to be so severe that he decided he must take the chance 'because he could do nothing else'. A few hours later the *Niña* dropped anchor in the outer port about four miles below Lisbon. Columbus at once sent a messenger ashore with a letter to King John explaining his plight and asking permission to continue upstream to the city, because he was afraid that some scoundrels, 'thinking that he carried much gold, might attempt some rascality' at his lonely anchorage. However, the king was away in the country and there was no immediate answer.

At anchor nearby was the most formidably-armed Portuguese warship that Columbus had ever seen, captained, as he was to learn, by Alvaro Daman. Next morning, she sent across an armed boat commanded by Bartholomew Diaz, the same Diaz who had made history by rounding the Cape of Good Hope. Diaz came alongside and demanded that Columbus go with him to give an account of himself. Columbus retorted proudly that as Admiral of the Sovereigns of Castile he would 'render

right:
Columbus on the bridge of his ship, by the Spanish artist Joaquin Sorolla y Bastida.
facing page, left:
Sea astrolabe of the late sixteenth century. Earlier astrolabes were used by Columbus and other navigators to ascertain their latitude at sea.
facing page, right:
A sandglass was the seaman's method of calculating the passage of time in the days of Columbus.
below:
A ship's compass of the sixteenth century, probably a slightly refined version of the type used by Columbus on his voyages.
facing page, below:
The First Landing of Columbus on San Salvador. An imaginative conception painted by Frederick Kemmelmeyer.

no accounts to any man and would not leave his ship except by compulsion', adding that it was the custom of the Admirals of Castile 'to die rather than yield either themselves or their men'.

Perhaps Diaz remembered Columbus from the old days, or perhaps his anger gave way to admiration for the defiance of the tattered, bearded figure on his storm-wracked little caravel. In any case peace was quickly restored, Columbus's *bona fides* were established to everyone's satisfaction, and soon afterwards Daman came aboard beaming goodwill and 'in great state, with drums, trumpets and pipes'.

Four days later, in response to an invitation, Columbus visited King John, who was staying at the monastery of Santa Maria das Virtudes about thirty miles from Lisbon. It must have galled the king that the enterprise which he had refused to support five years earlier had succeeded so brilliantly and that the fruits of it would go to Spain instead of to Portugal. But he gave no hint of his feelings and received Columbus 'with much honour and showed him much favour', and was generous in his congratulations. Columbus stayed two days, and when he left for Lisbon to rejoin his ship, the king said farewell to him 'with much affection'.

The *Niña* put to sea again on 13 March and reached Palos two days later. By an extraordinary coincidence the *Pinta* came in on the same tide only a few hours behind. However, this was not the *Pinta's* first landfall. Apparently she had escaped the storm which had so badly battered the *Niña* during her final run from the Azores, and had put in to Bayona, on the Galician coast in the north-west of Spain, probably during the last week in February. Not knowing whether the *Niña* had survived

and eager in any case to get in first with the news, Martin Alonso Pinzón had sent a messenger from Bayona across Spain to Ferdinand and Isabella at Barcelona, asking permission to visit them there and give them a first-hand account of the successful voyage. But the king and queen had replied curtly that they preferred to hear the story from Columbus.

Pinzón was a sick man, worn down by the hardships and exposure of the voyage home, and when he reached Palos and found the *Niña* already at anchor it was literally the last straw for him. While his ship was still furling sails and without reporting to Columbus or even greeting his brother Vicente, he was rowed ashore, made his way to his home outside Palos, went straight to bed and in a few days was dead.

Word from Lisbon had already reached Ferdinand and Isabella of Columbus's return, and from Palos he sent them an account of his voyage and sought permission to present himself at Barcelona. While he awaited a reply he spent about a fortnight at the monastery of La Rábida with his old friend and sponsor Fray Juan Pérez, and from there he went to Seville taking with him the ten Indians who had survived the voyage.

In Seville a week later he received a letter from the king and queen which to his great joy was addressed to 'Don Cristóbal Cólon, their Admiral of the Ocean Sea, Viceroy and Governor of the islands that he hath discovered in the Indies.' After congratulating Columbus on the success of his mission the letter went on: 'It is our will that that which you have begun with the aid of God be continued and furthered, and we desire that you come here at once; therefore for our service make the best haste you can, so that you may be timely provided

The monument at Granada to Queen Isabella and
Christopher Columbus.
above, left:
Christopher Columbus, a French painting depicting
the return of Columbus from his first voyage.
Musée de Luxembourg.

with everything you need ... to go back to the land which
you have discovered.'

Columbus at once drafted a memorial to the king and
queen which set out his ideas of how the new colony
should be governed. He considered that about 2,000
volunteer settlers should be sent, and that they should
be distributed among three or four towns, each with its
mayor and town-clerk and church and priests to convert
the Indians. Only licensed settlers should be allowed to
gather gold, and then only for part of each year so that
they would not neglect other business. All gold gathered
must be handed to the town clerk, and half would
become crown property.

The memorial was forwarded by courier, and Columbus then began his long overland journey to Barcelona,
taking samples of gold 'and many other things never
before seen or heard of in Spain'. With him, travelling
on horseback or in wagons, went some of his officers,
some servants and six Indians, clad in loinclothes, wear-
ing their ornaments and carrying spears and tame

parrots. All along the route people turned out in thousands to see the great hero and his entourage. There was
a brief stop at Cordova for Columbus to greet his sons
Diego and Ferdinand and his mistress Beatriz; then the
cavalcade continued on by way of Valencia and Tarra-
gona. Barcelona was reached late in April and crowds
of people flocked out of the city and lined the roads to
welcome the arrivals.

Next day, with great pomp, Columbus was received
by the king and queen in the presence of the entire court.
As he approached, Ferdinand and Isabella rose from
their thrones to greet him, and he knelt and kissed their
hands. Then at their request he sat next to their son, the
Infante Don Juan, called forward his Indians, exhibited
the things he had brought from the Indies, gave a long
account of his voyage and discoveries, and discussed
plans for his return. Later there was a service of thanks-
giving, and that night Columbus slept as a royal guest
after what had been without doubt the greatest day of
his eventful life.

CYCLURA Harlani. *Lesueur et Pitois.*

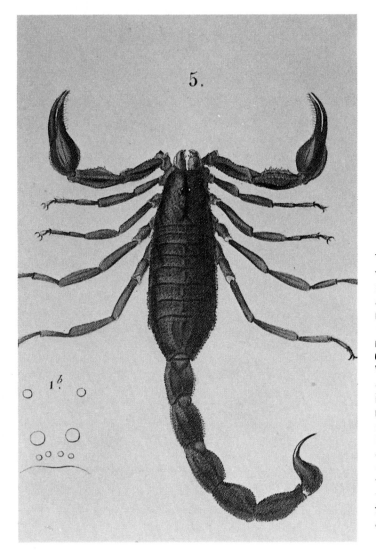

The birds of the New World and their melodies were 'exquisite', Columbus wrote, and he also noted that while the Indies abounded in lizards and other reptiles there were very few mammals to be seen. A scorpion of the West Indies can be seen on the left, and one of the more interesting lizards, the chameleon, below. On the facing page, bottom left, is another New World lizard, *Cyclura harlani*, and a hutia, *Capromys prehensilis*, one of the rare mammals, is on the facing page centre right. The Bahama redstar and the Cuban emerald, facing page top right, would certainly have been among the birds Columbus saw and described as exquisite, and other birds of the islands are the Cuban trogon, facing page, centre left, and the tody, facing page, lower right. All these pictures were originally painted by Ramon de la Sagra for his *Historia Fiscia, Politica y Naturel de la Ila de Cuba,* which was published in 1855. British Museum.

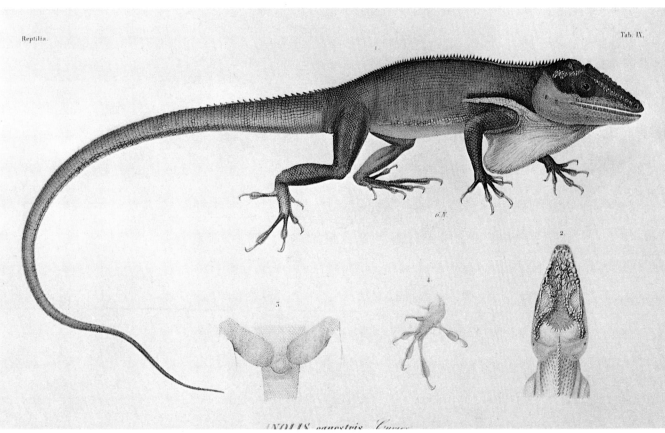

Reptilia.   Tab. IX.

ANOLIS eqnestris Curier

THE SECOND VOYAGE

Columbus stayed on for several weeks at Barcelona, lionised by courtiers who otherwise would have ignored his existence, flattered by the same scholars and sceptics who had once dismissed him as an ignorant and importunate adventurer. For a man of his proud and deeply sensitive nature the rewards of victory must have been sweet indeed.

Ferdinand and Isabella did not grudge him his triumph. At the same time they were anxious that he should leave as soon as possible on a second voyage, partly to consolidate their claim to Hispaniola by colonizing it and partly so that he could further explore the area. There was every need for haste. It was reported to them that King John of Portugal was already outfitting a fleet to sail westward, and only strong pressure persuaded him to postpone its departure for two months while the matter of Spanish and Portuguese spheres of influence was thrashed out diplomatically at Barcelona. The Portuguese proposed that all new lands south of the Canary Islands should belong to them, and that Spain should have everything to the north. The Spaniards countered by urging that the question be referred for arbitration to Pope Alexander VI (Rodrigo Borgia), who was himself a Spaniard and owed his recent election largely to the influence of Ferdinand and Isabella.

To hurry things along the king and queen made Don Juan de Fonseca, Archdeacon of Seville, jointly responsible with Columbus for organizing a second voyage. Fonseca, a shrewd businessman, was soon able to finance the venture and set to work at once to assemble a fleet of seventeen ships, to equip them with stores and everything required for a round voyage of six months, to enlist crews and prospective settlers, and to provide food, arms, seeds, plants, livestock, tools and the innumerable other items that would be needed for a new settlement.

Columbus was appointed Captain General of the Fleet and given a free hand to administer the new colony and to make further explorations, and was particularly instructed, so Las Casas states, to make sure whether Cuba was, as he still believed, part of a mainland or merely another island.

In June 1493 Columbus left for Seville, diverging briefly for a pilgrimage to the monastery of Guadalupe in the Estremadura mountains. This was in fulfilment of his vow made at the height of the storm on the way home. He also called at Cordova to see his mistress Beatriz de Harana and to take his sons Diego and Ferdinand with him to Seville. In the meantime he had written to his brother Batholomew, who was still in France, and to his youngest brother Diego, who was still working humbly in Genoa as a wool-weaver, telling them of the coming

In 1590 a German engraver, Theodore de Bry, working in London, began publication of a monumental series of accounts of voyages to the East and West Indies. They were published in parts, the texts were in Latin, and the engravings were by de Bry. Picture shows the title page of Part Four, published in 1594, which gave an account of the voyages of Columbus.

AMERICAE
PARS QVARTA.
Sive,

Infignis & Admiranda Hiftoria de reperta
primùm Occidentali India à Chriftophoro
Columbo Anno M. CCCCXCII
Scripta ab Hieronymo Bezono Mediolanenfe,
qui iftic ãnis XIIII. verfatus, diligẽter omnia obferva-
vit.

Addita ad fingula ferè capita, non contemnenda fcholia
in quibus agitur de earum etiam gentium idololatria.
Accefsit præterea illarum Regionum Tabula
chorographica.

Omnia elegantibus figuris in aes incifis expref-
sa à Theodoro de Bry Leodienfe, cive
Francofurtenfi Anno ɔ Ɔ Ɔ xciii Ad
Inuiſtis. Rudolphus II. Rom. Imperator.
Cum preuilegio S. C. Maieſtat.

Pope Alexander VI (Rodrigo Borgia), whose division of the New World into Portuguese and Spanish spheres of influence satisfied neither country. It was superseded by the Treaty of Tordesillas, of June 1494.

Ponce de León, who successfully subdued Puerto Rico and later discovered Florida, was a member of the crew on the second voyage of Columbus.

voyage and inviting them to join him.

Columbus and Fonseca were soon at odds, mainly because, having demanded a personal retinue which Fonseca considered excessive, Columbus referred the matter over Fonseca's head to the king and queen who ordered that his wishes be carried out.

During the next three months Columbus spent most of his time at Cadiz, whence the fleet was to sail, completing down to the last detail the organizing work which Fonseca had begun so ably. There were more arguments when Columbus found fault with some of the ships Fonseca had chartered, some of the people he had engaged and some of the stores he had ordered. Columbus's flagship, of about 200 tons, was officially named *Santa Maria* but became better-known as *Mariagalante*. There were two other ships of about the same tonnage, *Colina* and *La Gallega*, and the other fourteen were all small caravels, some of light draught for inshore navigation. Among them was the brave little *Niña*, refitted for her second transatlantic voyage.

This time there was no need to press unwilling seamen or to persuade other people to join the expedition. On the contrary about twice as many volunteered as the fleet could possibly carry, and Columbus's task was to sort out those who seemed to him most suitable. His choice was not always wise. Many he selected were young aristocratic adventurers, who lacked any aptitude for work and regarded the voyage as a free holiday from which they would return laden with gold and other spoil. The foremost of these gentleman volunteers was Alonso de Ojeda, who was to prove an excellent leader, an able fighting man and an important explorer in his own right.

In due course Columbus's brother Diego arrived from Genoa. He was, so Las Casas wrote, 'an honourable person, very discreet, peaceable and simple, and of good disposition', but these virtues were not necessarily those of a good leader, and in the event he was to be unequal to the heavy responsibilities thrust upon him. Regrettably for Columbus's sake, Bartholomew, a more mature

The departure of Columbus's fleet on his second
voyage. A Venetian version published in 1621.
There were actually seventeen ships in all.

and far more forceful character in every way, failed to
arrive in time, and when eventually he reached Cadiz
the fleet was already well on its way.

Among others who made the voyage were the chart-
maker Juan de la Cosa, who had also sailed on the first
voyage; Pedro de las Casas, whose son was to become
Columbus's biographer and historian of the New World;
Alonso Sanchez de Caravajal, mayor of the town of
Baeza, who was to prove a good and faithful friend to
Columbus; Juan Ponce de Léon, who was to earn later
fame as the discoverer of Florida; Francisco de Peñalosa,
in command of the expedition's armed forces; Mosén
Pedro Margarit, another high military officer; Dr Diego
Chanca, a physician of Seville; Michèle de Cuneo,
another old friend of Columbus's from Savona near
Genoa; and five priests led by Fray Bernardo Buil, a
Benedictine, whose particular job was to convert the
Indians to Christianity. Estimates of the total number of
people who sailed vary, but it was probably between
1,200 and 1,300. Columbus's own journal of the voyage

has long since disappeared, and the best first-hand
accounts of it which have been preserved come from Dr
Chanca and Cuneo.

Shortly before the sailing date it was rumoured that
King John of Portugal had already sent a ship westward,
but when an official protest was made about this he
denied all knowledge of it and undertook to send three
other ships to overtake and recall it. It is not known
whether any of these ever sailed and certainly Columbus
saw no Portuguese vessels, but Ferdinand and Isabella
took the rumour seriously enough to order him to keep
a strict look-out for them and to punish them appro-
priately if they were in fact in Spanish waters.

The departure of the fleet from Cadiz on 25 September
1492 was an occasion for great rejoicing and was accompanied by much ceremony.

It is of interest to note that on the following day Pope
Alexander VI finally came to a decision regarding Spanish
and Portuguese territorial claims and issued a Bull which,
in effect, gave Spain the right to all lands and islands,

discovered or still undiscovered, which might be found by sailing west or south. King John protested, with good reason, that this was unfair to Portugal. Intensive diplomatic activity followed, with the result that the Bull was ignored by both countries, and at Tordesillas on 7 June 1494 they concluded a treaty which was to ensure peace between them for a considerable time. In the terms of this a line was drawn from north to south 370 leagues west of the Cape Verde Islands, and Spain was given all land to the west of it and Portugal all to the east.

In favourable weather, Columbus made straight for the Canaries, and his fleet anchored at San Sebastian, Gomera, on 5 October, only ten days out. Fresh food was taken aboard, together with sheep, goats, pigs, cattle and fowls for breeding in the new settlement, and by 13 October with fair winds from the south-east the ships were on their way again on a west by south course. Columbus knew this would take them well south of Hispaniola, but on his way he was eager to examine and explore some of the Caribbean islands which he had been told about during the first voyage. In case any of the ships became separated the captains were given sealed orders how to reach Hispaniola and the fort at La Navidad. In fact, however, the fleet was not separated, and except for one sudden thunderstorm the voyage was completely uneventful.

On the evening of 2 November Columbus was so sure he was near land that he ordered the fleet to shorten sail for fear of overruning it during the night. His dead reckoning was so amazingly accurate that at dawn next day a high, mountainous island was in sight off the port bow. All hands on the flagship assembled on the quarterdeck and hymns were sung and prayer of thanks offered for so fast and safe a crossing. In fact the voyage from the Canaries had taken only three weeks, at an average sailing rate of about five knots, and Dr Chanca declared that even this time would have been bettered had the *Mariagalante* sailed as well as the other ships.

As it was a Sunday Columbus named the island Dominica. Soon afterwards a second, low and thickly wooded, was seen to starboard and he called this after his flagship. By noon four more islands were in sight, one of considerable size to which he gave the name Santa Maria de Guadalupe and, which is now known as Guadaloupe. Although Mariagalante had no harbour the fleet anchored overnight off its lee side, and next day Columbus went ashore, ordered a cross to be raised and took possession of all the islands in sight in the name of the king and queen.

The following day a landing was made on the south coast of Guadaloupe. Many natives were seen but they fled at the sight of the ships. An armed party of ten, under Diego Marquez, went ashore and headed inland 'for purposes of plunder' according to Cuneo.

Next day when they had failed to return Columbus became alarmed and sent four parties of fifty men each to look for them. No trace of them was found. Instead, in various villages from which the Caribs had fled the search parties found joints of human flesh ready for cooking, and rescued a number of young Arawak-speaking slaves of both sexes. The boys had been

right:
Destruction of the fort of Navidad and the massacre of its garrison by the cacique Caonabo.

The monument to Columbus at San Juan, Puerto Rico, commemorating his discovery of that island on his second voyage.

As the fleet continued west for Hispaniola many other islands were seen and named, including what are today known as Monserrat, Antigua, Nevis, St Kitts, Saba, St Eustatius, St Croix and a cluster of small islands which Columbus called the Eleven Thousand Virgins and are now known more simply as the Virgin Islands.

On 14 November the Spaniards had their first armed clash with Caribs. The fleet had anchored off St Croix, and a party of about twenty-five had been sent ashore for water. In an otherwise deserted village they had found and rescued some boy and girl slaves, and they were returning with these to their ship when a canoe appeared containing four men, two women and a boy. The natives, including the women, tried to fight it out with bows and arrows and two Spaniards were wounded, one of whom died later. The canoe was rammed and some of the natives were killed and others captured. One of the women had been taken personally by Cuneo and Columbus allowed him to keep her as a slave. She was young, naked and, her captor wrote, 'very beautiful'. The men, on the other hand, were described as 'of ferocious appearance, menacing and cruel'.

Five days later the fleet came to a much larger island and sailed all day along its south coast. Columbus called it San Juan Bautista (St John the Baptist) and on modern maps it appears as Puerto Rico. Two days were spent at anchor while water and fresh food were taken aboard, and on 22 November the ships crossed Mona Passage, separating Puerto Rico and Hispaniola.

Although Columbus was eager to reach La Navidad to relieve the garrison there, he realised that a better site would be needed for a permanent settlement, and on 25 November the fleet anchored in the harbour of Monte Cristi and a party was sent ashore to look for one. They returned with a report that they had found two bodies, too decomposed to be recognisable. Next day they found two more, one with a beard; and as the Indians were beardless Columbus feared, not without reason, that all four might be Spaniards.

La Navidad was reached on the evening of 27 November, too late for the fleet to enter the bay. Cannon were fired as a signal and Columbus's apprehension increased when there was no answer. During the night some natives came out in a canoe calling 'Almirante!', but they would not go aboard the flagship until Columbus had identified himself by the light of a lantern. Their leader, a cousin of Columbus's friend, the cacique Guacanagari, reported that some of the garrison had died of illness and others had been killed in a quarrel. The rest, they reported, were fit and well.

Early next morning this story was proved untrue when a party went ashore and found only the blackened, charred ruins of the fort. Under further questioning the chief's cousin declared that the whole garrison had been killed in an attack by Caonabó, the fierce half-Carib chief of Cibao, and that Guacanagari himself had been wounded while defending the fort and his own village.

Determined to get to the bottom of the affair Columbus marched on Guacanagari's village at the head of more than a hundred men, among them Dr Chanca. When the doctor removed the chief's bandage there was no sign of

castrated and were being fattened for eating and the chief function of the girls was apparently to bear babies, which were considered a particular delicacy.

Not surprisingly it was assumed that the missing party had already been killed and perhaps even eaten. There was intense relief, therefore, when they turned up four days later, exhausted and hungry but otherwise intact, and reported that they had become lost in the thick jungles of the interior. Although the island had no gold the Spaniards were impressed by its beauty and fertility, by its immense flocks of gaily-coloured parrots, and particularly by a luscious fruit which they were the first white men to taste and which we know as the pineapple.

One of Columbus's last acts before the ships sailed on 10 November was to order the destruction of every canoe that could be found, to hamper future slaving raids on Hispaniola. The rescued boys and girls, the latter 'very beautiful and plump', were taken aboard with a number of other released prisoners and a few Caribs who had been captured

cross the island by way of Santo Tomas to advise his brother of his impending return. Before returning to Isabella, Columbus planned a slave raid on Puerto Rico, but instead he went down with a high fever which, according to Las Casas, 'led to a lethargy that deprived him of sense and memory and almost proved fatal'. The Puerto Rico project was abandoned and the ships sailed direct for Isabella. When they arrived on 29 September Columbus was unconscious.

When he recovered consciousness he found that he was ashore and in bed and beside him, to his great joy, was his brother Bartholomew. It will be recalled that Columbus had written to Bartholomew in France inviting him to join the second voyage, but that he had arrived in Spain too late to do so. In response to another request from Columbus he had then taken the latter's sons Diego and Ferdinand to court where the king and queen had promised them appointments as pages to their son, the Infante Don Juan. Bartholomew had so impressed the Sovereigns that they had appointed him in charge of

three caravels which were to take supplies to Hispaniola, and in fact he had been in Isabella since June.

In Isabella and Hispaniola the situation did not straighten itself out, as Columbus had hoped, but became even more chaotic. Columbus's idea that Margarit and his men should explore the interior, living off the land, had not been a good one. Relieved by Ojeda at Santo Tomas, Margarit and about 350 men had ranged the island for several weeks, extorting food and gold from the natives, flogging and otherwise brutally ill-treating them, raping their women and suborning youths as slaves.

When word of this had reached Diego Columbus he had written to Margarit protesting against his behaviour. Margarit's answer had been to march with part of his force on Isabella, where he had won over some of the anti-Columbus faction including Fray Buil, seized the three caravels which Bartholomew had brought, and sailed with his supporters for Spain.

The men he had left in the interior had broken up into gangs and were still pillaging and terrorizing the

An otherwise unrecorded incident of the second voyage. Friendly natives, their chief smoking an oversized pipe, entertain Columbus and his officers to a meal of iguana and fruit. However, the atmosphere changes when Spanish priests destroy a native idol, and hostilities break out. The Blessed Virgin, hovering over the battlefield in a cloud, is of course on the side of the Spaniards. From a Venetian book of 1621.
below:
A Venetian artist's colourful but highly inaccurate version of a battle between Columbus's fleet and cannibals of one of the Caribbean islands.

Insulæ Canibalium

countryside, until in sheer desperation the natives had retaliated by ambushing and killing several of them.

As soon as Columbus was fit again his first act was to appoint Bartholomew as Adelantado or lieutenant-governor, and inevitably this further alienated the malcontents at Isabella. From then on his conduct was indefensible by any humane standards, even allowing for the times in which he lived. Instead of punishing the roving gangs left by Margarit as they so richly deserved he took the attitude that Spanish lives were sacrosanct, and decided to punish the frightened natives who had killed a few of them.

He sent strong parties inland with horses and mastiffs, and after some bloody clashes about 1,500 unfortunate men, women and children, many of them obviously quite innocent, were rounded up and brought to Isabella. By this time four more caravels, commanded by Antonio de Torres, had arrived with supplies; and as there was practically no gold or anything else of value to send home Columbus filled their holds with about 500 of his Indian

captives, men and women, to be sold in Spain as slaves. With his permission the settlers at Isabella helped themselves to another 600, and the rest, mostly women with young children, were turned loose.

When the caravels sailed on 24 February 1495 their passengers included Michele de Cuneo and Diego Columbus. Diego's task was to justify his brother at court against the prejudiced reports of Margarit, Fray Buil and others. According to Cuneo, during the passage home which took between two and three months about 200 of the Indians died and were thrown overboard, and most of the others were landed at Cadiz so debilitated and ill that there was little demand for them in the slave market. Within months almost all of them were dead.

Meanwhile in Hispaniola, Columbus had provoked a state of open warfare. Guatiguána, cacique of Magorix in the south-east of the island, who had already once escaped execution, rallied a force of some thousands of natives, intending to march on Isabella. Columbus learned of this and appointed Bartholomew and Ojeda his lieutenants,

right:
The tropic beauty of the Virgin Islands, discovered by Columbus, is exemplified in this picture of Road Harbour, Tortola.
below:
Some of the Virgin Islands, looking westward from the western end of Tortola.
right, above:
Caribbean club-head, with intricate decoration.
right, below:
Spaniards setting their fierce hounds on Indian captives. Engraving by Theodore de Bry.

In the picture on the facing page, centre, a drawing by Oviedo shows natives of Hispaniola washing gold. The metal was of little interest to the Indians but the Spaniards' greed for it brought horror to them. The other pictures, by Theodore de Bry, illustrate the tragedy. Facing page, below, the Spaniards receiving the gold tribute. This page, above, some Indians revenge themselves on a captured Spaniard by pouring molten gold down his throat. The final despair of the hapless natives is shown on the facing page, above. Unable to meet the gold tribute, they kill their children and then commit suicide in a variety of ways.
left:
Spaniards attacked by an Indian army as they raise a cross on the island of Hispaniola.

overleaf:
The Return of Christopher Columbus by Delacroix. This spectacular evocation is perhaps more Romantic than historically accurate but it catches the feeling of a great occasion to a remarkable degree. Toledo Museum of Art.

the island that men and women had to work long hours every day washing and panning in the mountain streams to gather their quarterly tribute. Many found the task impossible and took their own lives to escape the vengeance of their white masters. Others fled into the mountains where they were hunted down with dogs and killed or died of hunger and disease.

Meanwhile in Spain so many complaints had reached the king and queen regarding Columbus's administration that they decided to send Juan Aguado, who had captained a ship on the second voyage and so had personal knowledge of Hispaniola, to investigate them. In one of a fleet of four caravels Aguado reached Isabella in October 1495. Columbus was away in the interior but returned to the settlement as soon as he received word from Bartholomew. When he arrived Aguado had already assumed vice-regal power, and his attitude was so hostile that it became obvious to Columbus that he would need to return to Spain to defend himself in person.

He sailed from Isabella on 10 March 1496 in the *Niña*, accompanied by the *India*, a small, locally-built caravel in which Aguado was a passenger. Adverse winds early in the voyage forced both ships to put in to Guadaloupe for water and food and shore parties became involved in a pitched battle with Caribs who opposed their landing. There were casualties on both sides before the natives fled. Cadiz was finally reached on 11 June after a tedious passage of three months. Of thirty Indians whom Columbus had taken with him only a few survived. Among those who died on the voyage was Caonabó.

THE THIRD VOYAGE

The years and the ordeal of the voyage home had left their mark on Columbus. When he stepped ashore he was exhausted and ill, and although only forty-five his hair and beard were now snow white. The court was somewhere in northern Spain, and while he awaited a royal summons Columbus recruited his strength and health at Los Palacios, a small town near Seville, where he was a guest of the local curate, Andres Bernáldez. His life there was quiet and on the few occasions he ventured into the streets of Seville he wore the simple brown habit of a Minorite friar.

Late in July he received a letter from the king and queen inviting him to visit them as soon as convenient. Hoping no doubt to repeat his triumphant progress and arrival at Barcelona after the first voyage, Columbus again organized a cavalcade of natives decked in gold ornaments and carrying cages of brightly-hued parrots and other exotic products of the Indies. But by now so many disillusioned colonists had returned from Hispaniola that the Spanish public had become sceptical, and for all Columbus's brave show his progress inspired very few cheers.

At Valladolid he learned that the court was on its way to Burgos about eighty miles away, and he hurried there to see Diego and Ferdinand, who were still in the royal service as pages to the Infante Don Juan. When the king and queen arrived a few days later they received him graciously, but neither they nor the court were greatly impressed by the gifts he had brought. Aguado's adverse report and the attacks of his many enemies had apparently

done Columbus less harm than he had feared, and it was agreed in principle that he should return to the Indies to consolidate the Spanish rule there and to make further explorations.

But for the time being the attention of the Sovereigns was concentrated on political matters and particularly on arranging marriages for their children that would strengthen Spain's position in Europe. Hispaniola was no longer a glittering prize and Columbus's promises of gold beyond the dreams of avarice had worn a bit thin. It is not surprising that his demands for more ships and men were now low on the list of royal priorities.

On 3 April 1497 at Burgos the Infante Don Juan was married to the Archduchess Margarita of Austria, and three weeks later, with this momentous event off their minds, the king and queen authorized Columbus to go ahead with plans for his next voyage. His original rights, titles and privileges were confirmed, as was the appointment of Bartholomew Columbus as Adelantado of Hispaniola. He was authorized to take out 300 colonists including farmers, gardeners, artisans and miners at the Crown's expense and to make land grants to deserving individuals.

As few Spaniards now had any taste for life in the Indies, pardons were offered to criminals who would volunteer to accompany Columbus, and the length of their service in Hispaniola would be determined by the seriousness of their crimes. Arrangements for the voyage were again entrusted to Juan de Fonseca, now Bishop of Badajoz, who this time found difficulty in raising finance

Columbus with his two sons, Diego and Ferdinand, and his mistress, Beatriz Enriquez de Harana, a peasant's daughter living in Cordova.

In addition to smoking tobacco the Indians also took snuff. Snuff-holders such as this one were used for ceremonial purposes.

for the venture and, because of his hostility to Columbus, went out of his way to harass and obstruct him.

Months of frustration followed. As 1497 dragged on, two events occurred which must have greatly heightened Columbus's anxiety and impatience. In July the Portuguese captain Vasco da Gama sailed from Lisbon with orders to round the Cape of Good Hope and sail on to India, where he was to establish a permanent trading post. Two or perhaps three months later came an even more disturbing report that John Cabot, a Genoese of Columbus's own age whom he may well have known in childhood and who was now in the employ of Henry VII of England, had found a practical northern sea-route to Asia and had actually landed at several places on its north-western coast.

In fact what Cabot had done had been to rediscover that part of north America which the Norsemen had found and briefly colonized five hundred years before. His voyage began from Bristol on 2 May 1497 in a small ship, the *Mathew*, with a crew of eighteen which included

Cabot's son Sebastian. After a hazardous voyage of more than seven weeks landfall was made at Cape Breton Island, now part of the Canadian province of Nova Scotia, where Cabot went ashore, raised the standard and claimed possession of the territory for England. Farther north he landed on what is now Newfoundland. Then, with good following winds he hurried back to report his momentous news and to receive on his arrival on 6 August a hero's welcome and the king's personal thanks. With a promise of several much larger ships, Cabot immediately began planning a second voyage.

Early in 1498, while Columbus was still fuming at the interminable delays to his own plans, Cabot actually turned up in Seville hoping to recruit seamen for his new venture. There is no record that the two met, but it is hardly likely that they failed to, and Cabot's personal confirmation of his achievement must have been galling indeed to Columbus. For the sake of his peace of mind it is as well that news travelled so slowly in those days, for in fact Cabot was well on his way by the time Columbus

far right:
One of the earliest-known maps of Hispaniola, now in the University Library of Bologna, Italy. It was possibly drawn by Columbus's brother Bartholomew, a noted map-maker of his day.
below:
England's years of seafaring greatness were still to come when King Henry VII sponsored a voyage by the Genoese seaman John Cabot which resulted, in 1497, in the rediscovery of Newfoundland, first settled by the Norsemen five centuries earlier.

overleaf:
The departure of John and Sebastian Cabot from Bristol, 1497.

right, below:
The West Indian parrots which Columbus took home from his first voyage caused a sensation in Spain; no one in Europe had ever seen the like of these gaudy creatures. Among the many birds of this type indigenous to the area are the red and yellow macaw *(Macrocercus aracanga)* and the blue and yellow macaw *(Macrocercus ararauna),* shown here in the superb drawings by the famous English artist Edward Lear. British Museum.

MACROCERCUS ARACANGA.
Red and Yellow Maccaw.

MACROCERCUS ARARAUNA.
Blue & Yellow Maccaw.

Columbus in chains after his arrest by Bobadilla.
Painting on a marble-topped table in the Mariners'
Museum, Newport News, Virginia.
right:
The coat of arms adopted by Columbus in 1502
and incorporated in his Book of Privileges.
far right:
The reception of Columbus by Ferdinand and
Isabella on his return from his third voyage.
From a painting by Francis Jover.
Museo Civico Navale, Genoa.

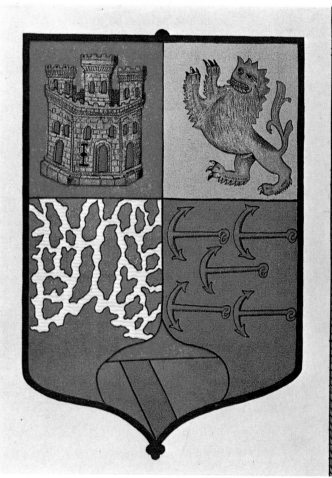

Vasco da Gama, the great Portuguese navigator. His voyage to India, following the rounding of the Cape of Good Hope by Bartholomew Diaz, established the sea route to the east and founded the Portuguese empire there.

left:
Giovanni Caboto, a Genoese. Better known as John Cabot, he searched for a northern route to Asia in the employ of King Henry VII of England. The lands he actually discovered were Newfoundland and Nova Scotia. From a painting in the Palazzo Ducale, Venice.

finally sailed. On this occasion Cabot took a more northerly route by way of Greenland, and after revisiting the areas he had discovered on his first voyage, he coasted southwards as far as what is now Maryland. Having found no signs of an Asian civilization, and with provisions critically low, he was forced to turn for home. When he reached England late in 1498 he was seriously ill and the great sailor died soon afterwards.

In the meantime the *Niña* and *India*, in both of which Columbus owned a half-share, had already left Cadiz for Hispaniola with much-needed supplies, but Columbus was still waiting round in Seville in such a state of frustration because of Fonseca's deliberate delays, that on one occasion, so the story goes, his anger exploded against the bishop's accountant, one Ximeno de Breviesca, whom he knocked down and then soundly kicked as he sprawled on the deck.

At long last all was ready, and in the final week of May 1498 the six vessels which Columbus was to command made their way downstream from Seville and anchored at the mouth of the Guadalquivir. There Columbus joined them, and on 30 May his third voyage began.

Three of the ships, all caravels, were to sail direct to Hispaniola with men and supplies; the others, comprising a flagship about the size of the *Santa Maria* the name of which has been lost and two caravels, *El Correo* and *La Vaqueños*, were to explore farther south than Columbus had been before and where he had heard rumours of an extensive mainland.

The caravels for Hispaniola were captained by men whom Columbus could trust implicitly – his old friend Alonso Sánchez de Carvajal; Pedro de Harana, the brother of his mistress; and Giovanni Antonio Colombo, one of his cousins from Genoa. Columbus himself commended the flagship and his other captains were Pedro de Terreros, who had been with him on the first voyage, and Hernan Péres.

The main accounts of this voyage are from Columbus himself, and are contained in a letter to Queen Isabella and in a surviving abstract of his journal in the hand of Las Casas.

The long delay in sailing had not only strained Columbus's patience but had also affected his health, and when he left Spain, he wrote, he was 'much fatigued', and suffering from arthritis and ophthalmia. He was about forty-seven years old at this time.

After a brief call at Madeira, where Columbus was given 'a fine reception and was well entertained', the fleet sailed on to Gomera in the Canaries. Here they separated, the three caravels making direct for Hispaniola and Columbus, with his flagship and two consorts, continuing further south to the Cape Verde Islands. From here he sailed south-west for about 450 miles until he reckoned he was in about the same latitude as Sierra Leone, and then he turned due west.

Progress was slow for the trade winds were light and soon faded to a dead calm. For awhile, he told the queen, 'the heat was so intense and the sun's rays so hot that I thought we should have been burnt'. For eight days his ships drifted in the doldrums; then a favourable and strong wind came in from the east-south-east, and for the rest of the crossing the ships scudded along exhilaratingly under full sail, logging an average journey of about 180 miles each day.

At noon on 31 July land was seen ahead. It had the appearance at first of three small, high islands, but on closer approach these were seen to be part of what was apparently one large island. Columbus called it Isla de la Trinidad, Island of the Trinity. Landfall had been made at its south-eastern corner, and the ships altered course to sail along its south coast. A bay into which several small streams poured was seen and parties were sent ashore for water.

Two days later there was another landing and friendly contact was made with the Indians. They were certainly not Asians as Columbus had hoped; nevertheless, he found them attractive and described them to the queen as 'very graceful in form, less dark than others in the Indies, and with long, straight hair'. They were also, he added, 'more shrewd and intelligent and less timid' than those of Hispaniola.

below:
Half a century after the death of Columbus England was challenging Spanish power in the New World. Foremost among her great seamen was Sir Francis Drake, scourge of the Caribbean, conqueror of the Armada, and the first Englishman to sail round the world. He died in the West Indies in 1596.
right:
One of the great English seamen and explorers of the Elizabethan age was Sir Walter Raleigh, founder of the colony of Virginia. Having lost favour with the queen he was imprisoned for many years, and a disastrous expedition to the Orinoco in search of gold led to his execution in 1618.

95

above:
A nineteenth-century watercolour of Cabot's ship, the *Matthew*, off Cape Race, Newfoundland.

right:
A Victorian artists impression of the landing of John Cabot in Newfoundland. With him is his son Sebastian, also a famous seaman and explorer.

During the next nine days Columbus explored what he called the Gulf of Paria, west of Trinidad, never suspecting that its western shore was in fact part of the mainland of South America, nor that the numerous streams which poured into the gulf were the delta of one mighty river which was later to be named the Orinoco. The rise and fall of the tides in the gulf was particularly great, and there was much turbulence with treacherous currents as river and sea water met.

Several landings were made on the north side, now known as the Paria Peninsula, which Columbus mistook for another island and called Isla de Gracia. During one landing, following his usual custom Columbus had a great cross raised, and in the presence of uncomprehending natives he took possession of the area for Spain.

Columbus's health had not improved during the voyage. Arthritis was still troubling him and sleeplessness had so inflamed his eyes that he was almost blind. In this feverish state he conceived a bewildering theory which he expounded at length in his letter to the queen.

The earth, he decided, was not altogether round after all but had one protuberance which he likened to the nipple of a woman's breast, so that ships which encountered it 'went on rising smoothly towards the sky', and this explained why the climate in the neighbourhood of Trinidad was so much more temperate than in Sierra Leone which was in about the same latitude.

At the peak of this protuberance, he further declared, lay the Terrestial Paradise from whence rose the world's principal rivers; Ganges, Euphrates, Tigris and Nile.

On 13 August the ships left the gulf through its narrow northern strait which because of its fearsome tide-rip Columbus called Bocas del Dragon, or Dragon's Mouth, and for two days they sailed westward along the north side of Paria Peninsula. As the coastline continued to show no break Columbus revised his opinion and decided that it was probably part of 'a very great continent', and if this were so 'it was a marvellous thing'.

Yet his mind was so filled with abstruse geographical theories and illness had so impaired his judgement that

top:
A *duho*, or wooden stool, in the form of a human figure. Found at Santo Domingo.

above:
Two stone rubbers from the West Indies, one in human form and one representing a bird.

right:
Jamaica is rich in traces of its former Arawak-speaking inhabitants. This wood carving of a male figure was found in a cave in Carpenter's Mountains.

instead of continuing to pursue this vitally important exploration he decided that his presence in Hispaniola was urgently needed, and within sight of an island he called Margarita he ordered the ships to turn north. The decision was doubly unfortunate, for closer examination would have revealed that he was in fact leaving a pearl-fishing area so rich that it could have yielded him a hundred times the wealth of the gold in Hispaniola.

During Columbus's long absence from the island and on his orders, Bartholomew Columbus had begun to establish a new capital called Santo Domingo at the mouth of the Ozama River on the south-east coast. It was a much more eligible site than Isabella, healthier, with fertile soil, a permanent water supply and a well-protected harbour; and today, known once more as Santo Domingo it is not only the oldest but still one of the most important cities of the Caribbean, capital of the Dominican Republic.

When Columbus reached the new capital on 31 August it was as yet only half-built, partly because of lack of labour but mainly because Bartholomew had had to concentrate most of his energy on other matters. He had never been popular as acting-governor and feeling against him had culminated in a rebellion led by Francisco Roldán, the chief justice of the island. When Columbus arrived Roldán and his followers were in the south-western province of Xaragua, where by specious promises Roldán had won the friendship of the cacique Béhechio and his beautiful sister Anacoana, the widow of Caonabó.

By an unfortunate miscalculation the three supply caravels which Columbus had sent ahead from the Canaries had overshot Santo Domingo by several hundred miles and had eventually reached the coast near Roldán's headquarters. Unaware of the rebellion the captains welcomed Roldán aboard, supplied him with arms and provisions and allowed their own men to go ashore. Most of these were released criminals and Roldán had little trouble in persuading them to desert, with the result that his original gang of about seventy rebels was

Vuelbeel Alm^{te} y alla quemada la Torre de Nabidad y los Castellanos muertos.

del Pre^{te}

Indias Don Xpoual Colon

Almirante delas Primero

El Alm^{te} descubre la ysla dela Trinidad y tierra firme

ENMA
en la Im
Re
de Nicola
fra
Año

above:
Discovery by Columbus of the island of Trinidad
(shown with three peaks) and the mainland of
South America, with inset portrait of Columbus.
From a history published in Spain in 1730.

right:
The Genoese seaman Sebastian Cabot in later life.
As a young man of twenty-one he had been with
his father at the discovery of Newfoundland.

very considerably augmented and now a strong force.

Roldán's defection was only one of many problems Columbus inherited from his brother. Discontent was as rife as ever in Santo Domingo and throughout the island. Few Spaniards would work when they had slaves to do it for them, and their manner had become more arrogant than ever. Many had died, many more were ill and at least 150 were down with syphilis. Most of the island's surviving natives, excluding those in Xaragua, were now thoroughly cowed but although they laboured hard, few were able to meet their quarterly gold tribute and the system had virtually broken down. Apart from slaves there was practically nothing of value that Columbus could send home, and when two of his ships left for Spain he crammed their holds with unfortunate natives he had rounded up.

As he had few troops on whose loyalty he could rely, Columbus decided against dealing firmly with Roldán and instead tried to placate him. With Carvajal acting as intermediary an agreement was eventually reached and

signed by Columbus on 21 November, in terms of which all the rebels were pardoned and promised transport home within fifty days with as many concubines and slaves as they chose to take. When no ships became available in the specified time Roldán brazenly raised his terms. He now demanded to be reinstated as chief justice and that land grants, with the right to enslave all natives who lived on them, should be made to all rebels who elected to remain on the island. Again Columbus was obliged to capitulate.

In the meantime news of Columbus's discoveries in the Paria area had reached Spain. Alonso de Ojeda managed to get hold of Columbus's chart and realising what a priceless opportunity he had missed persuaded Juan de Fonseca to grant him a licence to make further explorations in the area; in the autumn of 1498 with companions who included the map maker Juan de la Cosa and a Florentine adventurer named Amerigo Vespucci he sailed from Spain. From Paria, Ojeda coasted westward about 700 miles and established

EFFIGIES · SEBASTIANI · CABOTI
ANGLI · FILII · IOHANIS · CABOTI · VENE
TI · MILITIS · AVRATI · PRIMI · INVEN
TORIS · TERRÆ · NOVÆ · SVB · HENRICO · VII · ANGL
IÆ · REGE

SPES · MEA · IN · DEO · EST

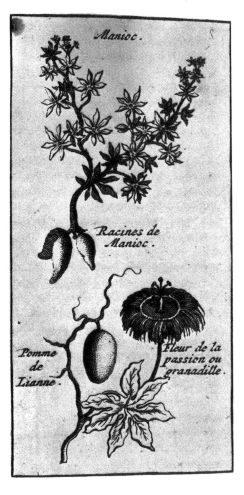

An eighteenth-century French artist's impression of some of the flora and fauna of the West Indies. The natives on the slope of an active volcano, facing page, upper right, are hunting 'devil birds'. A 'great spider' and a soldier crab are among the creatures to be seen on the same page, bottom.

left:
Two products of the West Indies — a manioc (or cassava) plant, the roots of which were ground into a sort of flour; and a passion fruit and passion flower.

above:
A mangrove tree of the West Indies, described by an eighteenth-century French artist as a wild fig.

beyond doubt the existence of a very considerable mainland.

He found the rich pearl fisheries which Columbus had missed in the Margarita area, and went on to discover the islands of Bonaire, Curaçao and Aruba and the extensive Gulf of Maracaibo. In the latter he saw several native waterside villages built on piles, and he named the area Venezuela, or Little Venice. At Cabo de la Vela on the west side of the gulf he left the mainland and turned north for Hispaniola. Carefully avoiding Santo Domingo he landed on the coast at Xaragua where he clashed, although not seriously, with Roldán; then he continued on to the Bahamas, filled his holds with slaves and returned to Spain.

In theory Columbus still held a monopoly on all exploration in the Indies, and the fact that Fonseca could afford to ignore this by licensing Ojeda's voyage clearly reflected the extent to which Ferdinand and Isabella had lost confidence in the ageing Admiral. The point was further underlined when Fonseca approved two more voyages. The first of these was made by Columbus's former pilot Peralonso Niño, who visited the Paria area and returned to Spain with a fortune in pearls; and the second by the *Niña's* old captain Vicente Pinzón, who explored part of the north-east coast of what is now Brazil and discovered the mouth of the Amazon River.

By early 1500 Columbus must also have learned of Cabot's second voyage and of Da Gama's return to Lisbon in September 1499 from his triumphant voyage to India, and the knowledge of these two achievements

A curious stone figure found at Santo Domingo.
From the Salisbury Collection and now in the
British Museum.

A stone pestle of the West Indies in the shape of a human head. Six and a half inches high, it was probably used for grinding maize, the Indian corn.

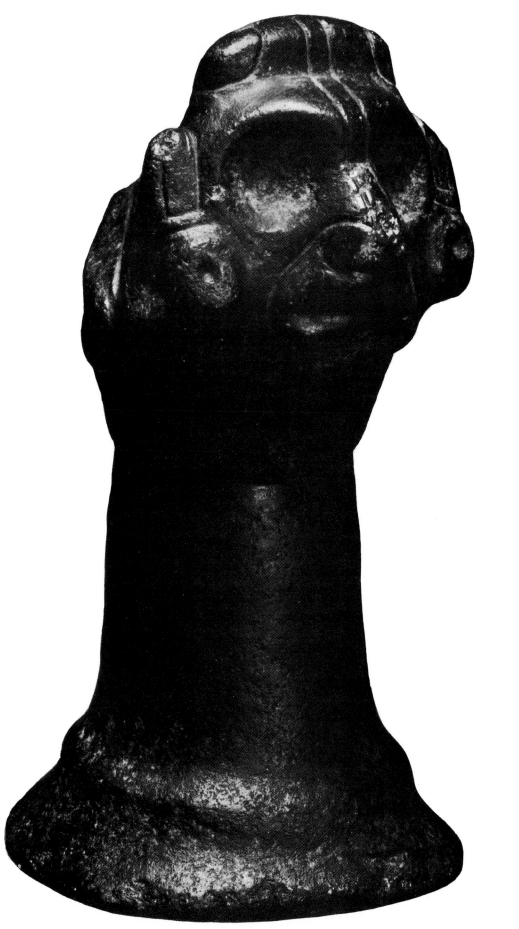

would certainly have come as an additional bitter blow to his pride.

On Hispaniola the state of affairs had shown no improvement. Even though Columbus had managed to pacify Roldán at much cost to his own prestige there were soon other rumblings of revolt. The first challenge to his authority, led by a young aristocrat named Fernando de Guevara, was smartly checked, and Guevara, who had planned to marry Anacoana's daughter Higuamota, who was said to be even more beautiful than her mother, was arrested and put in jail.

A second revolt led by Adrian de Moxeca, one of Roldán's lieutenants, had more drastic consequences. While Columbus was at Concepción, one of the chain of forts he had built in the interior, he learned that Moxeca was marching against him with a gang of rebels. With only a dozen men on whom he could rely Columbus emerged from the fort, surprised the rebels at night, captured Moxeca and several others and routed the rest. Moxeca was publicly hanged in Santo Domingo, his companions were imprisoned in irons, and Columbus and Bartholomew hunted down those who had escaped, killed some and hanged others on the spot.

After that there was peace of a kind but the reputations of the Columbus brothers were now irreparably damaged and in addition to their failure as administrators they were condemned as 'tyrants, unjust men and cruel enemies, who rejoiced in shedding Spanish blood'. In Spain, as disgruntled colonists continued to return, many in rags and reduced to beggary, feeling against Columbus reached such a pitch that his sons Diego and Ferdinand, who were now pages to the queen, were so vilified that they hardly dared appear in public.

Most important of all perhaps, the colony was costing Spain huge sums in ships and supplies. Columbus had failed utterly to make good his promises of untold wealth from the Indies, his exploratory work on the second voyage had been so inefficient that he had missed the rich pearl fisheries of Paria, and the cargoes of slaves he sent home in lieu of other wealth not only yielded a poor financial return but deeply offended Isabella, who had said categorically that she wanted no natives in Spain who had not already been converted to the Catholic faith.

The queen's patience reached breaking point when yet another shipment of slaves arrived, many of them young girls either pregnant or with newly-born babies. She ordered them to be returned to Hispaniola at once, and agreed with Ferdinand that the time had come for a full-scale inquiry into Columbus's administration. As commissioner they chose Francisco de Bobadilla, an official of the royal household who had given long and faithful service.

Bobadilla's powers were to be absolute. He was authorized to arrest all rebels and to seize their effects; to dispense justice as he saw fit; to adjust all grievances, and to take over all forts, arms and royal property. He was given blank warrants signed by the king and queen so that he could deal with any other situations that might arise, and also a letter from them instructing Columbus to obey him in all things.

Bobadilla sailed in one of two caravels which left Spain

in company in July 1500. With him in one were his advisers, officials, servants and a strong bodyguard. In the other were the slaves who were being returned on Isabella's order.

When the ships reached Santo Domingo on 23 August Columbus and Bartholomew were away in the interior hunting down rebel remnants, and their brother Diego was in nominal charge of the capital. The first thing Bobadilla saw was a gibbet by the waterside from which hung the bodies of seven Spaniards; and when he landed and presented his credentials to Diego he was told that five more were to be hanged next day. Bobadilla acted promptly and drastically.

Diego was arrested, fettered and imprisoned aboard one of the caravels. The citizens of Santo Domingo were assembled and Bobadilla read his commission to them and warned them that disobedience of his orders would be severely punished. He took over the citadel, installed himself in Columbus's house, impounded the admiral's papers and effects, helped himself to

what gold he found there, released all prisoners including those due for execution, and sent messengers to find Columbus and Bartholomew with orders that they were to return at once to Santo Domingo.

Columbus was the first to appear. Without being given a chance to speak in his own defence or even to know what charges there were against him, he was arrested, put in irons and imprisoned in the citadel. Bartholomew, still at large with a strong armed force, would willingly have fought it out with Bobadilla, but Columbus sent him a note begging him not to and he submitted quietly. He too was fettered and put in jail.

Bobadilla had no trouble gathering evidence against Columbus; on the contrary almost every citizen of Santo Domingo came forward with one complaint or another. Among these were that Columbus had forced them to work at hard and unnecessary labour, that he had reduced their rations and restricted their liberty, that his punishments had been excessive and often unjust, that he had treated the natives cruelly and prevented their conver-

sion, that he had hidden treasure which rightly belonged to the Sovereigns, and that in general he had abused his office for the enrichment of himself and his family. No doubt much of the evidence was perjured or at least suspect. Nevertheless, Bobadilla decided that at least some of the charges must have substance, and he ordered that the Columbus brothers be sent home to Spain and there put on trial.

Early in October, still in chains, Columbus was taken from the citadel and led through a hooting, jeering crowd.

He and Diego were put aboard the caravel *La Gorda*. It is uncertain whether Bartholomew went with them, but more probably he sailed in another ship. As soon as the caravel had cleared the harbour her captain, Alonso de Villegio, offered to remove the Admiral's chains, but Columbus refused. 'My Sovereigns commanded me to submit to Bobadilla's orders', he said. 'By his authority I wear these chains, and I shall continue to wear them until they are removed by order of the Sovereigns'. And so he returned to Spain.

THE FOURTH VOYAGE

With fair weather and following winds *La Gorda* made fast time and reached Cadiz late in October. People on the waterfront stared in amazement as Columbus, now a venerable, white-haired figure, half-crippled by arthritis, stepped ashore still in chains and accompanied by a jailer. As word of his degradation spread there was a mounting wave of indignation throughout Spain.

Certainly there were hundreds of returned colonists ruined in health and pocket who could testify that his administration of Hispaniola had been far from perfect, but this did not necessarily mean that he was a criminal. After all he had discovered the place and put it on the map, and to most people he deserved credit for that.

During the voyage home Columbus had written a long and emotional letter to Doña Juana de la Torre, a lady of the court and a close friend of the queen's. As soon as the ship arrived this was smuggled ashore and sent by messenger to the court in the hope that it would get there before Bobadilla's damning report and that it would be passed on to Isabella. Pending his trial, if there was to be one, Columbus was spared the indignity of imprisonment and was allowed to stay at the Carthusian monastery of Las Cuevas in Seville. Diego, who had a leaning towards the priesthood, was probably with him and it is likely they were soon joined by Bartholomew.

Certainly they were together about six weeks later when an order came from Isabella that they were to be freed at once and given 10,000 ducats, equivalent to about £8,000 in modern currency, so that they could travel to the court, which was then at Granada, in a manner befitting their status. Consequently when they arrived on 17 December they wore new and rich clothes and were accompanied by a small retinue.

Columbus's meeting with his Sovereigns was an emotional occasion. He wept as he kissed their hands and was still weeping when he declared that any errors he may have made had been through lack of experience rather than want of zeal, and assured them before God of his everlasting loyalty and love. Isabella was deeply and visibly affected and even Ferdinand was not unmoved. Together they assured Columbus that they retained the fullest confidence in him, hinted that Bobadilla would be recalled and punished, and ordered the immediate restoration of all his income and rights. On the subject of his reinstatement as viceroy, however, they were less forthcoming. They said this would be reconsidered.

As usual nothing happened for a long time. Columbus had a happy reunion with his sons Diego, now twenty, and Ferdinand, now twelve; and if his long wait in Granada achieved nothing else it at least considerably improved his health. With time to spare he compiled a curious Book of Prophecies, consisting of passages from the Bible and other sources which could possibly be

Juan de la Cosa, mapmaker and seaman, who made the first map of the West Indies in 1500.

interpreted as predicting the discovery of the New World, with the inference that he was the man whom God had chosen both to accomplish this and to restore the Holy Sepulchre to Christendom. He sent a copy of this book to the king and queen with a letter in which he urged them to undertake a crusade to the Holy Land. The idea appealed to the mystical side of Isabella, but Ferdinand had other, more practical things to think about.

In the meanwhile much had happened and was happening on the far side of the Atlantic. Early in 1500 a Portuguese fleet of thirteen ships commanded by Pedro Alvarez Cabral had left Lisbon for India to consolidate da Gama's gains there and, sailing far westward off course, had accidentally reached the coast of Brazil on 24 April. A few days later Cabral had gone ashore at what is now Porto Seguro, about 600 miles north of Rio de Janeiro, and had taken possession of the land for Portugal, naming it Vera Cruz, the Land of the True Cross. Rodrigo de Bastidas had explored the coast west from Venezuela to the Gulf of Darien; a Portuguese captain, Gaspar Corte-Real, had followed Cabot to Newfoundland and examined much of the nearby mainland coast; and at least three other navigators, including Amerigo Vespucci, had cruised the South American coast, as far south, according to Vespucci's own highly-suspect account, as latitude 52° to the present Patagonia.

Although huge gaps remained to be filled in, the evidence of a western continent was now overwhelming, and the first mapmakers to delineate it, although inaccurately, was Juan de la Cosa in his *Mappemonde* of 1500, on which incidentally Columbus was portrayed in the dress of St Christopher.

Columbus's hopes of being restored to his old position were finally dashed on 3 September 1501 when the Sovereigns announced the appointment of Don Nicolas de Ovando as governor of the islands and mainland of the Indies except for certain parts of the mainland over which Vicente Pinzón and Alonso de Ojeda respectively were to have control. Columbus realized that protest would be futile. However, he won the right to send an agent to Santo Domingo to demand a reckoning from Bobadilla and to collect what was due to him; and when Ovando left Cadiz on 13 February 1502 with a fleet of thirty ships and caravels Columbus's old and trusted friend de Carvajal sailed with it to carry out that task.

Knowing that he could no longer return to Hispaniola as viceroy and perhaps secretly even a little relieved, Columbus's thoughts turned again to the sea and he decided to seek royal backing for yet another voyage of discovery. Against mounting evidence to the contrary he still believed that Cuba, which had not been revisited since 1494, was part of the Chinese mainland.

He now conceived the idea that between Cuba and the Gulf of Darien there must be a sea passage westward through which he could reach India and continue thence, following da Gama's route in reverse, back to Spain, thus becoming the first man in history to sail round the world. It was a noble and daring ambition for a man of fifty-one in dubious health, and it was just possible that his theory could be right. Isabella and Ferdinand had gambled on him once and won, and they decided to do so again.

Pedro Alvarez Cabral, the Portuguese who discovered Brazil in 1500. The Treaty of Tordesillas gave Portugal sovereignty over a vast area of South America.
right:
The female, fruit-bearing papaw tree, or papaya, drawn and engraved by the Rev. Griffith Hughes, who visited Barbados in the eighteenth-century, for his *The Natural History of Barbados*, published in London in 1750.

Plate 15

To His most serene Highness
The Prince of Hesse
This Plate is humbly Inscrib'd,
&c.

HONI SOIT QUI MAL Y PENSE

Plate 15

G. D. Ehret. delin. & sculp.

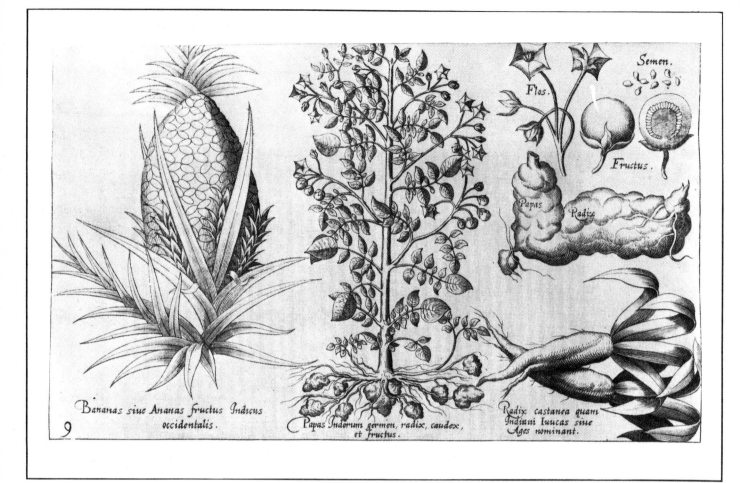

Bananas siue Ananas fructus Indicus occidentalis.

Papas Indorum germen, radix, caudex, et fructus.

Radix castanea quam Indiani Iuucas siue Ages nominant.

9

above:
Fruit and vegetables of the New World, from a
Venetian book of the early seventeenth-century.
Left, pineapple; centre and top right, West Indian
potatoes; lower right, yucca (or manioc) roots.
right:
Banana palm with fruit, drawn by Griffith Hughes.
It is still uncertain whether bananas are indigenous
to the West Indies or whether they were introduced
after 1492.
far right:
Products of the West Indies — Indian corn, Guinea
corn and sugar-cane. Sugar-cane is not indigenous
to the area, and African sugar-cane was introduced
by Columbus on his second voyage.

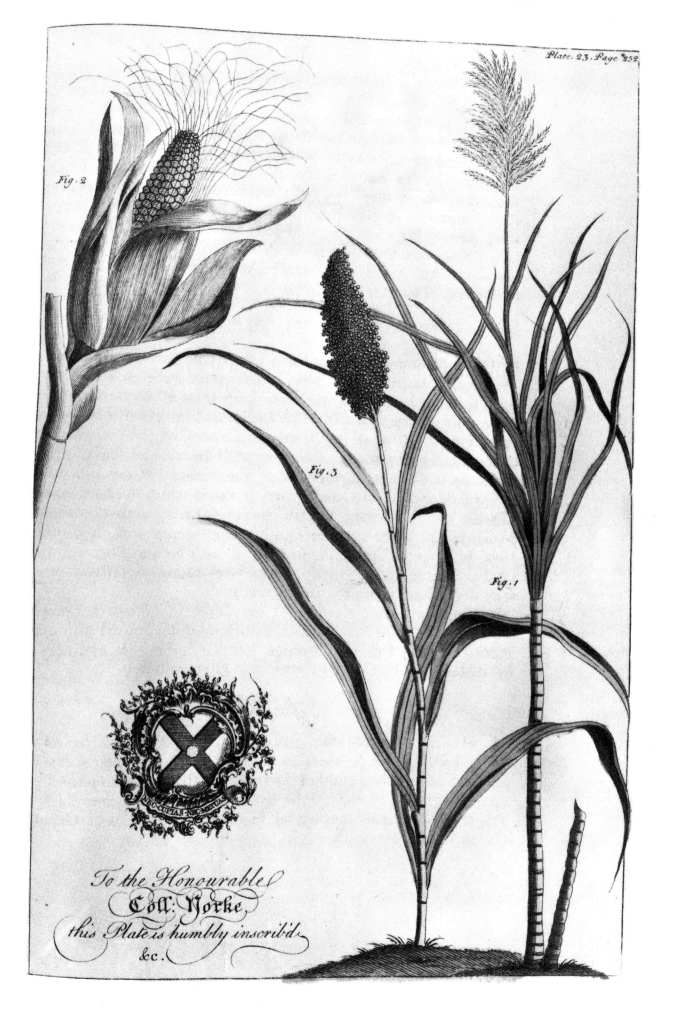

Fig. 2

Fig. 3

Fig. 1

NEC·COPIAS·NEC·MVTVAS

To the Honourable
Coll: Yorke,
this Plate is humbly inscrib'd
&c.

115

below:
How to catch a turtle. A picture from a sixteenth-century book showing how to render helpless this valuable source of food found in the New World.
right:
Spaniards and Indians caught in a hurricane on Hispaniola. Engraving by Theodore de Bry.

Tortüe qui veut pondre.

Maniere de tourner les Tortües.

Four small caravels were chartered and Columbus was given the money to outfit and crew them. This time, however, there were to be restrictions. Columbus was to do no private trading. He was to take an official accountant, Diego de Porras, who was to have charge of all gold, silver, pearls and precious stones that might be found. He was not to carry off natives as slaves; and he was forbidden from calling at Santo Domingo on the outward voyage, although he could do so on the way home if it should be necessary.

Perhaps even more important to Columbus than the voyage itself was the Sovereigns' assurance that his privileges would be preserved intact for himself and his heirs. While his ships were being fitted and equipped Columbus made several copies of the Book of Privileges which he had begun before his third voyage. Two were sent to a bank in Genoa, one he left with his son Diego, and one he deposited for safekeeping in the monastery of Las Cuevas. In addition he made a new will which ensured that his mistress Beatriz de Harana would not be left in want.

Of the four caravels, Columbus was to sail in the largest, known simply as *La Capitana*, with Diego Tristan, a trusted former shipmate as captain. The *Santiago* was captained by Francisco de Porras, brother of the accountant; *El Gallego* by Pedro de Terreros; and the *Vizcaino* by Bartholomew Fieschi, a Genoese whom Columbus had known in the old days. Columbus was to be accompanied in the flagship by Ferdinand, now aged fourteen, and Bartholomew was to sail in the *Santiago*. Brother Diego, who had had more than his fill of foreign travel, was to stay at home and, with the court's blessing, to study for the priesthood. In all the four ships carried about 140 people, most of them young and many still in their teens.

The tiny fleet put to sea on 11 May 1502 and reached the Canaries nine days later. Wood, water and fresh food were taken aboard, and on 26 May the Atlantic crossing began. Conditions were even better than usual. The weather was good, the trade wind was strong and constant, and in the remarkably short time of three weeks landfall was made at Martinique, where Columbus allowed his people to rest and refresh for three days. There was a brief stop at Dominica on the way north, and by 24 June the ships were in sight of Santo Domingo.

Although Columbus had been forbidden to call there on the outward voyage he had good reasons for wishing to do so. There were letters to send home; he hoped to be able to exchange the *Santiago*, which had proved a poor sailer, for another caravel; and more urgently he sought shelter from a hurricane which instinct and experience warned him would blow up in the next two or three days.

Inside the harbour the fleet which had brought Ovando from Spain was about to leave on the return voyage, and when Columbus sent Torreros ashore to ask permission to enter he also advised the governor to keep his ships in port until the hurricane had blown over. Ovando's reply was disdainful. He refused Columbus's request and ignored his warning. The same evening the fleet put to sea and Columbus sailed westward hoping to find shelter.

The homeward-bound ships had barely cleared the island and were crossing Mona Passage when the hurricane screamed in and hit them from the north-east The chaos was indescribable. Most of the ships went down with all hands, a few were driven ashore and smashed up, and three or four limped back to Santo Domingo in a sinking condition. More than 500 men were drowned, among them Columbus's old enemies Bobadilla and Roldán, his old friend Antonio de Torres, and the cacique Guarionex who was on his way to Spain as a captive.

Gold worth 200,000 castellanos (about £300,000), gathered at an appalling cost in native lives, was also lost, including a single nugget worth 3,600 castellanos, the largest ever found in the Indies. Of the whole fleet only one small caravel, the *Aguja*, weathered the hurricane and reached Spain. By a stroke of irony, or perhaps of poetic justice, Alonso de Carvajal was aboard her with about £6,000 worth of gold which he had managed to squeeze out of Bobadilla on Columbus's behalf.

Columbus's own fleet survived intact. Before the

hurricane struck they anchored close under the land, and although three of them were driven far out to sea and separated they suffered comparatively little damage and no casualties. A few days later all four of them were together again.

Columbus set a course south-west from Hispaniola against contrary winds with occasional calms. On 30 July he reached an island called by the natives Bonacca, the largest of a group which lay about thirty miles off the coast of what is now Honduras. The inhabitants were friendly but they had neither gold nor pearls, and Columbus did not linger. The mainland was reached at Cape Honduras, and on 14 August Columbus went ashore, raised a cross and took possession of the country for Spain. Most of the natives had their ears bored to carry large ornaments, so Columbus called the area Costa de las Orejas, the Coast of the Ears.

During the next four weeks the fleet coasted slowly east in appalling weather and against strong and persistent headwinds. Columbus wrote to his Sovereigns that

Three stone pestles with human heads. They vary in height between six and seven inches.

A West Indian ritual object in stone, decorated with a seated figure. Its precise purpose is not known but it is likely to have been a ceremonial dagger.

he had never experienced a tempest so violent or that lasted so long.

'In all this time', he told them, 'the ships lay exposed, their sails rent, their rigging and other equipment destroyed, and my people broken in health, continually swearing to be good and vowing to go on pilgrimages and even hearing one another's confessions.' Columbus himself became seriously ill, and the one thing that continually heartened him was the fortitude and steadfast courage of young Ferdinand.

On 14 September the coast turned sharply south. What had been headwinds now became following winds, and the long ordeal was over. The customary hymns were sung and prayers of thanks offered, and Columbus named the cape they had rounded Gracias á Dios, Thanks to God. The run down the coast of present-day Nicaragua was easy and pleasant, and as soon as a suitable anchorage was found Columbus called a halt for ten days to rest his men and repair his ships. The natives seemed amiable but they carried bows, arrows and spears, and only

strong, well-armed parties went ashore. They returned with enthusiastic reports of a rich countryside teeming with deer, pumas, monkeys, boars, wild turkeys, great flocks of parrots and other wild life, and, of more interest, of 'a great palace of wood in which were some tombs with carved wooden tablets'.

The caravels were on their way again on 5 October, with Columbus still eagerly seeking a sea passage to India. Two days later they anchored in what is now Chiriqui Lagoon, Panama. Though there was no sign of a strait Columbus was delighted to find that most of the Indians wore gold discs round their necks worth up to ten ducats each which they happily exchanged for hawks' bells. Understandably the trade in these was brisk, and from then on, as Ferdinand wrote later, 'we began to go trading all along the coast'.

During ten pleasant days spent at anchor Columbus learned from the local Indians that the name of the country was Veragua, that it was an isthmus, and that in nine days' march across the mountains he would reach

Spanish attack on an Indian stockade. Engraving by Theodore de Bry.

another sea and a native province called Ciguare, where there was an immense quantity of gold. Columbus had no difficulty identifying this with Chiamba, Marco Polo's name for Cochin-China, and he calculated that India was only a further ten days' sail away.

However, there was still the problem of how to get there, for the Indians were emphatic that there was no strait either in Veragua or beyond. After six more weeks of futile sailing along the coast Columbus reluctantly agreed that they must be right. On 26 November at a spot which he called The Retreat he finally abandoned the search and turned back. From then on his only interest was in gold.

By the beginning of 1503 the caravels were again off the Veraguan coast, and early in January they anchored in the mouth of a river which Columbus called the Belen. Shore parties went prospecting in a nearby river and returned with so much gold that it was decided Bartholomew should remain there with *La Gallega* and about eighty men to form a small colony. Until now the local

Indians and their cacique Quibian had been friendly enough, but when they saw huts and a storehouse being built and realized that the strangers meant to stay their attitude changed, and only firm and courageous action by Bartholomew prevented a mass attack on the new settlement.

Meanwhile the bar at the river entrance had become so shallow that Columbus had to wait until heavy rains fell in early April for him to put to sea. He may as well have stayed in port for adverse winds ruled out any chance of reaching Hispaniola as he had planned, and he was obliged to anchor a few miles offshore to await a favourable change.

A few days later a boat commanded by Diego Tristan went ashore for water. When it reached the settlement a battle was in progress between Bartholomew's men and the Indians. One Spaniard was killed and several wounded, and the Indians were driven off with great loss. Tristan pursued them up the river in his boat but was ambushed and he and all but one of his crew were

below:
A rare double-bladed stone axe found on the Mosquito Coast of Costa Rica, which Columbus explored on his fourth voyage. About twelve and a half inches high, it could have been used as a weapon or for ceremonial purposes.
right:
A stone figure from Guetar, on the eastern coast of Costa Rica.

killed. This man escaped by swimming underwater, and managed to reach the settlement.

In fear of another mass attack Bartholomew withdrew his men to the beach behind a barricade of casks, and they were still there three days later when a messenger arrived from Columbus asking anxiously for news of Tristan. It was obvious that the settlement would have to be abandoned. As *La Gallega* was unable to cross the shallow bar, everything of value in her was transferred by raft to the other caravels and she was then scuttled.

As a direct course for Hispaniola was still out of the question Columbus decided to sail eastward until he came to a certain point from whence he hoped to reach the island in one long tack. The three caravels were now in appalling condition, their timbers so rotten and worm-riddled that 'all the people with pumps, kettles and other vessels were unable to bail out the water'. Of the three the *Vizcaina* was the worst, and at Porto Bello, which Columbus had discovered and named about a year earlier, she had to be abandoned. On 1 May the remaining vessels, *La Capitana* and *Santiago*, left the coast somewhere in the Gulf of Darien and sailed as nearly due north as the wind would permit.

But Columbus had made faulty calculations, and instead of reaching Hispaniola he made landfall in the dangerous maze of the Queen's Garden on the south coast of Cuba. After one futile attempt he realized it would be impossible to beat eastward against the wind and instead stood off to the south for Jamaica. On 24 June he reached the north coast and anchored near St

Ann's Bay in what is now Don Christopher's Cove, and here he lashed his waterlogged, crumbling ships together and beached them.

The man who most proved his worth and courage in this critical time was Diego Mendez, who had succeeded Tristan as captain of *La Capitana*. First he negotiated successfully with the local caciques to provide a regular and ample supply of food. Then he volunteered to make his way to Hispaniola in a canoe with a native crew. On his first attempt he ventured ashore near the eastern end of the island and was captured by Indians from whom he escaped and made his way back to the cove. Soon afterwards he set out again this time with two large canoes, the second commanded by the Genoese Bartholomew Fieschi.

They took with them twelve Spaniards and twenty Indian paddlers, and Bartholomew Columbus and a well-armed shore party escorted them as far as the end of the island.

The distance from the eastern tip of Jamaica to Cape Tiburon at the western tip of Hispaniola is about 110 miles, and the crossing, in intense heat and against the current, took an agonizing four days. At Cape Tiburon, Fieschi proposed that he should return to let Columbus know all was well while Mendez continued along the coast to Santo Domingo, but not a man, Spaniard or Indian, would face the ordeal again and Fieschi had no choice but to continue on.

On their way east they learned from natives that the governor, Ovando, was in the Xaragua area with a strong

DRÍD
orenta.
al
e Rodriguez
no
de 1720

El Almte descubre con grandes
Tormentas la costa de Veragua

Adelantado delas Indias ✝ Don Bartme Colon hermno del Almte primero

Franciscus Poraz   Christophorus Columbus

left, above:
The landing of Columbus and his men opposed by
the natives of Veragua, on the coast of Central
America. The inset portrait is of Bartholomew
Columbus. Illustration from a history published
in Spain in 1730.
left:
Spanish priests and soldiers being massacred by
Indians. Engraving by Theodore de Bry.

above:
A battle between Columbus's men and a rebel force
led by Francisco de Porres at the anchorage in
Jamaica. Engraving by Theodore de Bry.

force putting down a local revolt. Mendez therefore
abandoned his canoe, struck inland and found Ovando at
his headquarters. Ovando seemed little concerned over
the plight of Columbus and his marooned men and
insisted that he must first deal with the rebellious
Xaraguans. This he did in the most bloody manner,
killing hundreds of them and hanging or burning alive
their leaders, among them the beautiful Anacoana.

While this slaughter went on Mendez was detained at
headquarters, and only after seven months as a virtual
prisoner was he allowed to make his way overland to
Santo Domingo. What Fieschi was doing in this time is
not known, but he certainly survived to return to Spain
for he was a witness to Columbus's last will and
testament.

In Jamaica, as the months passed without word, all
hope that the canoes had reached Hispaniola was abandoned. Many of the stranded men blamed Columbus for
their predicament, and early in January 1504 the growing
discontent of a section of them flared into an open mutiny

led by Francisco and Diego Porras. Columbus, who was
in bed with arthritis, barely escaped being murdered, and
the mutineers, who totalled about fifty, seized ten canoes
and set out for Hispaniola. On their way eastward they
robbed and plundered coastal villages at will and killed
any natives who opposed them. After three attempts to
cross to Hispaniola had failed they gave up the idea and
roamed about the island instead.

In the meantime affairs were going badly with Columbus and his faithful followers. By now the Indians in the
area had more hawks' bells and beads than they knew
what to do with, and they saw no point in labouring to
bring in more food to trade for useless toys. Faced with
an imminent threat of starvation Columbus countered
it with typical ingenuity. From a book by the astronomer
Regiomontanus he learned that a total eclipse of the
moon had been predicted for 29 February 1504, and he
sent a messenger to invite the caciques and other leading
Indians to a conference on that day. When they had
gathered he told them that God was angry because they

123

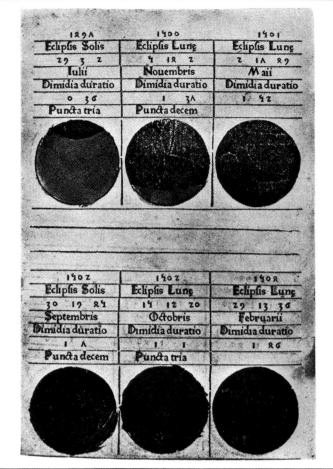

had ceased bringing in food and intended to punish them, and as a sign of this He would blot out the moon that night. Some of the natives were sceptical, some afraid. Fortunately for Columbus the astronomer's prediction was correct, and as the moon rose it was already partly in eclipse. Columbus retired to his cabin and stayed there until the eclipse was at its full. Then he emerged, told the now terrified natives that he had been praying to God, and that God had agreed not to punish them so long as they continued to bring in food supplies. This they promised readily to do; and as the eclipse waned their fear gave way to intense relief and they overwhelmed Columbus with thanks for his intercession.

About a month later to the great joy of the stranded men a small caravel entered the harbour. However excitement changed to bitter disappointment when they learned she had not come to rescue them but merely to deliver two casks of wine and some salt pork and to bring a message from Ovando that a larger ship would be sent for them when one became available. Columbus sent a dignified reply to the governor and the caravel left.

At least they could now console themselves that their plight was known and that they would be saved sooner or later. Columbus sent a messenger with the news to the Porras mutineers and magnanimously offered them a general pardon. Instead, however, they chose to fight it out; and in a pitched battle which the natives watched with great interest they were routed by the loyalists, led by Bartholomew Columbus. Several mutineers were killed, several others including Francisco Porras were

above:
A page of a book on astronomy predicting (bottom right) a total eclipse of the moon on 29 February 1504. Foreknowledge of this event enabled Columbus to terrify the natives of Jamaica into providing food for himself and his stranded crew.
above, left:
A spectacular example of Arawak carving. A seated figure, probably of a god, found in Jamaica. It is of wood with teeth of shell inlay and is twenty-seven inches high.

captured, and a few were hanged. Next day the survivors surrendered unconditionally and were freed on swearing to obey and be faithful to Columbus.

Late in June a caravel chartered by Mendez appeared and after just over a year in Jamaica Columbus and his men were taken aboard. The voyage back to Santo Domingo against adverse winds and currents was long and arduous, and the capital was not reached until 13 August. Columbus was welcomed warmly and with a great show of friendship by Ovando, who had done practically nothing to help him, but the governor revealed his true feeling when he freed and showed favour to the Porras brothers.

At Santo Domingo another ship was chartered, and in September Columbus, his brother, his son and about twenty others sailed for home. The passage was long and stormy, and it was not until 7 November 1504 that Columbus finally set foot on Spanish soil.

THE
AFTERMATH

Time had passed Columbus by. On this occasion his return to Spain went almost unnoticed. By the general public he was already half-forgotten; to those at court he was merely a boring old man who had failed yet again to make good his promises and who no longer merited any interest. Isabella, the one person who might have welcomed him, was seriously ill, in fact on her death-bed, and she died at Medina del Campo on 26 November.

Even without the queen as an ally Columbus was determined to get what he considered his due under the terms of the Royal Capitulation of 1492, but he was too ill and exhausted from the long ordeal of the voyage to travel to court. Instead he rented a house in Seville and presented his case through his son Diego, now an officer of King Ferdinand's guard, to whom he wrote a series of letters outlining his various claims and giving detailed instructions how they should be pressed.

Diego was a dutiful son and as his father's heir it was in his own interest to do all he could. But in fact he achieved little for if all Columbus's claims had been granted they would have made him the richest man in the world, and not without reason Ferdinand regarded some of them as preposterous. It is of interest to note that one of these many letters to Diego was carried by Amerigo Vespucci, who had been summoned to court to discuss matters of navigation. 'He is a very honourable man to whom fortune has been adverse as it has to many others', Columbus wrote to his son. 'He is desirous of doing all in his power for me, so see what he can do to profit me and strive to have him do it.'

When Diego failed to make any progress Columbus sent other spokesmen to the court, which was then at Segovia, among them his brother Bartholomew, his son Ferdinand and his agent Carvajal; and when they did no better he determined to go himself. But his health was little improved, and several months passed before he was able to travel. Eventually he made the long journey in easy stages by mule, reaching the court in May 1505.

Ferdinand was friendly enough at first, but his manner became evasive when Columbus asked for the restitution of his honours and dignities and the payment of the large sums which he considered due to him. At one stage Ferdinand sought to compromise by offering Columbus a rich estate in the province of León if he would renounce his titles and revenues, but he refused to accept this.

From Segovia the court moved to Salamanca and then to Valladolid, and in spite of his steadily deteriorating health Columbus went with it, still arguing, still pressing his claims and still getting nowhere. At last he had to admit defeat. 'I have done all that I could do', he wrote. 'The rest I leave to God, whom I have ever found helpful in time of need'.

Then one final though remote chance presented itself. The Infante Don Juan had died years ago, soon after his marriage, and with Isabella's death the crown of Castile had passed nominally to her daughter the Infanta Juana and her husband the Archduke Philip of Hapsburg. But Juana had had a series of mental breakdowns and she and her husband were living abroad; Ferdinand had assumed the regency in their absence.

The house at Valladolid in which Columbus died.
He followed the court from city to city until his
strength gave out, then he sent his son
Bartholomew to plead his cause.

The Death of Columbus, by Francisco Ortega.
There are many pictures which depict this event:
Ortega's is perhaps the most successful in
suggesting the desolation of a man who died
believing himself both misjudged and ill-used.

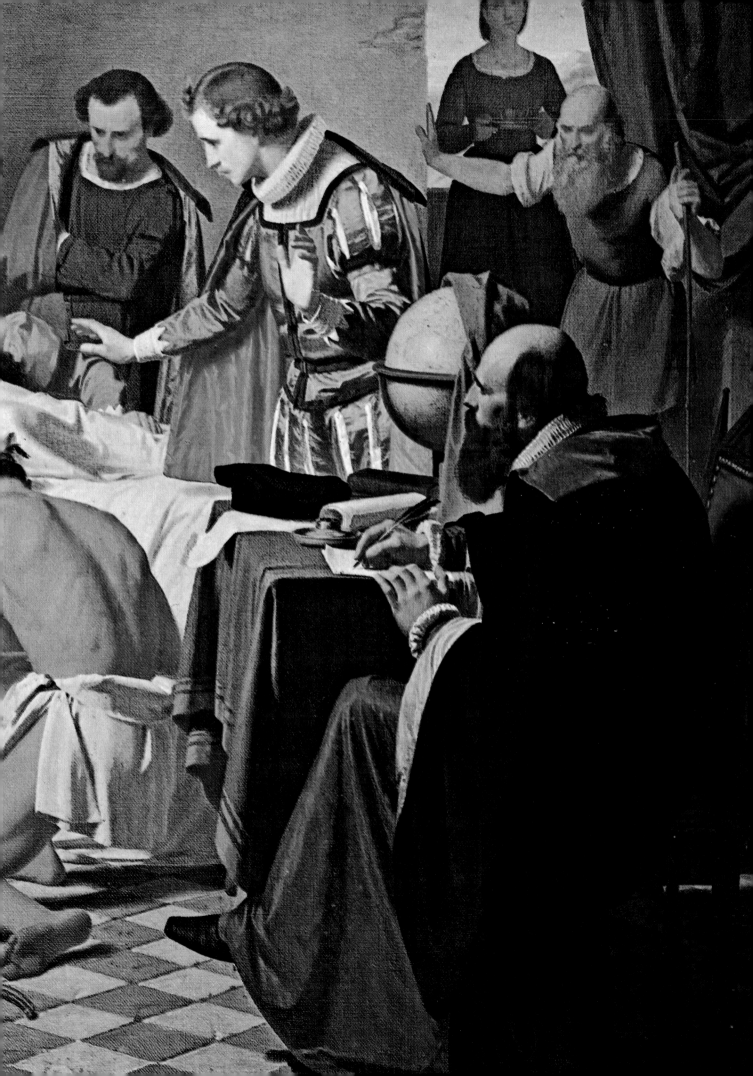

right:
Diego Columbus's palace at Santo Domingo after
its restoration in 1957. It is in Spanish Renaissance
style and contains twenty-two rooms. The main
vestibule on the ground floor measures fifty by
twenty-one feet, and the upper floor has a vice-
regal reception room of the same dimensions.
below:
Santo Domingo. The ruins of Diego Columbus's
palace in the late nineteenth century.
far right:
Ferdinand Magellan, the Portuguese explorer who,
in the service of Spain, undertook to travel west to
reach the east, thus proving incontrovertibly that
the world was round and the Americas a separate
continent. He did not live to complete his epic
voyage; of a fleet of five ships only the *Vittoria*
limped home to Spain, two years later, and Magellan himself was killed by natives in the Philippines.
right, below:
Map by Johannes Contarenus and Franciscus
Rosellus, dated 1506, delineating the West Indies
and part of America.

There were fears that Ferdinand would marry again and produce an heir, and with support from the nobles of Castile the royal couple landed at Corunna in April 1506 to claim their inheritance – a futile action as it happened for Philip died the same year, and Juana went mad, and the nobles had no choice then but to confirm Ferdinand as regent of Spain.

However, this was still in the future. Columbus remembered Juana only as a child who had listened eagerly at the time of his triumphant appearance at Barcelona to his wonderful stories of the New World, and he convinced himself that through her he might yet obtain what he believed to be his rights. He was now far too ill to travel from Valladolid to the royal camp, so he sent Bartholomew to plead his cause.

Bartholomew was still away when Columbus's condition became much worse. That was on 19 May. Realizing that the end was not far off he dictated and signed a long codicil to his will in which he confirmed his son Diego as sole heir to all his property and privileges. There were substantial legacies for his two brothers and his son Ferdinand and Diego was directed to provide adequately for Beatriz de Harana.

Next day it was clear that he was dying. A priest was summoned, a Mass was said and Columbus was given absolution. Among those at his bedside were his brother Diego, his sons Diego and Ferdinand and his old friends and seagoing companions Diego Mendez and Bartholomew Fieschi. Soon afterwards, it is said, he sent for the chains which symbolized the degradation he had suffered

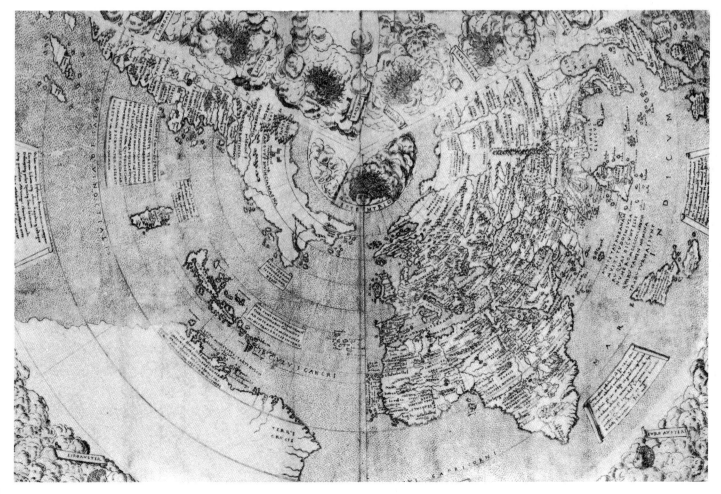

right:
A beaker from Tiahuanaco, a civilisation
that preceded the Incas in the highlands of
Peru (seventh century A.D.), and belongs to the
Kemper Collection.
far right:
Cortez. The great mural by Orozco in Mexico City is
a bitter comment on the achievements of the
Conquistadors. Personal glory and national prestige
invariably resulted in the brutal oppression of the
American Indians.
below:
The first page of Columbus's *Book of Privileges*,
which he compiled in 1502 before his final voyage.
Of several copies made the one shown is in the
Naval Museum, Pegli.

Vasco Nuñez de Balboa, the conquistador who
discovered the existence of the Pacific Ocean in
1513. He took formal possession of it for Spain.
Remarkable both for his courage and humanity,
he won the friendship of the Indians. He fell
foul of Spanish intrigue and was beheaded for
treason in 1513.

above:
Francisco Pizarro, the conqueror of the Inca
empire. He was in his sixties when he siezed the
last Inca, Atahualpa, in 1533. In the same year he
captured the Inca capital, Cuzco, and secured its
tremendous treasures for Spain.
right:
The statue of Amerigo Vespucci in the porch of the
Uffizi in Florence.

under Bobadilla, and he was clutching these in his hands
when he died.

Columbus's death excited little general interest, and
his funeral was modest. After temporary burial at Valladolid his body was transferred to the monastery of Las
Cuevas at Seville, and there it remained for thirty years.
In 1536 it was removed again, this time across the Atlantic
to Hispaniola where it was reburied beside the grand
altar of the cathedral of Santo Domingo, and here it
remained in peace for more than 250 years. When Hispaniola was ceded to France in 1795 the relics, now
reduced to dust and a few bones, were again exhumed
and transferred to the cathedral of Havana, from whence
once more they were returned to Seville after Spain had
lost Cuba to the United States in the war of 1898. Some
historians have expressed doubt about whether the
remains moved from Hispaniola were in fact those of
Columbus – but on the available evidence it seems
probable that they were.

The huge sums which Columbus had claimed were,

of course, never paid. Nevertheless Ferdinand approved
Diego's right to the title of Admiral and continued to
advance his career. In 1509, soon after his marriage to
Doña Maria de Toledo, a lady of the court, he was
appointed governor of Hispaniola.

He stayed there long enough to prove that, unlike his
father, he was an able administrator, and to build the
massive castle the ruins of which still stand. He died in
1526, aged forty-six, leaving a son Luis who proved to be
a bitter disappointment. The present heir and represen-
tative of Christopher Columbus belongs to the Lar-
reatagui family, descendants through the female line,
and he still retains the now meaningless title of Admiral
and Duke of Veragua.

When Don Diego went to Hispaniola in 1509 he was
accompanied by his half-brother Ferdinand. But Ferdinand's voyage with his father had satisfied his appetite
for adventure; his taste was for scholarship, and after
only six months at Santo Domingo he returned to
Europe. In the following years he travelled extensively

AMERIGO VESPUCCI

On the right can be seen the country near Malinalco in the valley of Mexico. To Cortez and his men, crossing country like this and with only the experience of colonial Cuba behind them, the existence of the brilliant Aztec civilisation came as a tremendous shock. What was never learned by them, or by Pizarro and his men, was that the civilisations they destroyed were simply the last in a long line of succeeding cultures. They never suspected the existence of the ruins of Monte Albán (eighth century A.D.), facing page, or of Tula, above, where at the same period the Toltecs were lords of Mexico.

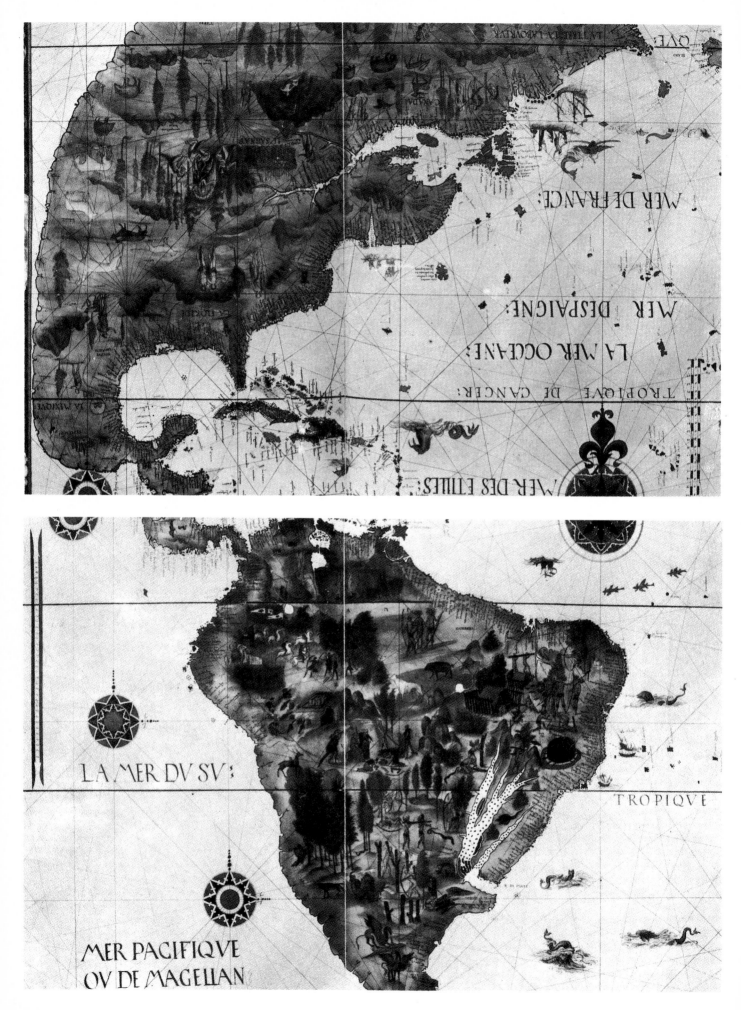

LA TERRE A LABOVRERE

QVE

MER DE FRANCE

MER D'ESPAIGNE

LA MER OCEANE

TROPIQVE DE CANCER

MER DES ETILLES

LA MIXIQVE

LA MER DV SV

TROPIQVE

MER PACIFIQVE
OV DE MAGELLAN

Amerigo Vespucci, by Stradanus. While he
hardly deserved to have the New World named
after him Vespucci was a considerable
explorer and discovered the mouth of the Rio de
la Plata. He also evolved a system for
computing nearly exact longitude, and
calculated the circumference of the earth at the
equator to within fifty miles.
left, above:
A detail from a sixteenth-century map of the world
made for Henry II of France, showing North
America as it was known at the time.
left, below:
South America, from the same map.

overleaf:
Seville. The city and port in the sixteenth
century, with the River Guadalquivir curving
away to the left. Painting by Sanchez Cuello.

through Europe and became a noted man of letters. He settled in Seville in 1525 where he accumulated a priceless library of 15,000 books, some of which had belonged to Columbus. The work by which he is remembered, a history of the Indies incorporating a biography of his father, was finished during 1538, and he died the following year.

Some time after Columbus's death Bartholomew, whose standing at court continued to be high, was sent on a mission to the Pope concerning new voyages of discovery. During Don Diego's governorship he went back to Hispaniola, and he died there in 1514. There is no record that Bartholomew ever married, and his only known descendant was an illegitimate daughter born to him in 1508.

Diego Columbus, the quiet and gentle one of the family, eventually realised his ambition to be a priest. His life from then on was obscure, and when he died in 1515 he was buried in the monastery at Las Cuevas beside his famous brother.

Because of the vagueness of Columbus's background and the complexity and apparent paradoxes of his character there has been a great deal of scholarly argument over the years about him and all aspects of his life. He was certainly a man with many faults but it is easy to find plausible excuses for these. It is equally easy to emphasize his faults and to denigrate the extent of his achievement. It has been said, for instance, that he did not know where he was going, that he had no idea where he was

when he got there, and that he never realised where he had been. Strictly speaking this is true.

It is also true that he did not actually discover America, and that if he had not found the New World someone else most certainly would have within a few years. In spite of all this, however, the indisputable fact remains, as his distinguished modern biographer, Samuel Eliot Morison, has pointed out, that in addition to being the greatest seaman and navigator of his age he did more to direct the course of history than any person since the Emperor Augustus Caesar.

Although Columbus clung stubbornly until his death to the belief that Cuba was a mainland peninsula of Asia it had been apparent to others for some time that this could not be so. On La Cosa's map of 1500 it is shown as an island, and any lingering doubt was removed in 1508 when Sebastian de Ocampo proved it so by sailing right round it.

From then on Spanish expansion was swift. Jamaica was occupied in 1509; in the same year Columbus's old shipmate Juan Ponce de Léon began his conquest of Puerto Rico; and two years later the great island of Cuba was invaded and eventually subdued by Diego Velasquez.

These conquests were savage and cruel. African slaves, many of them born in Spain, had first been taken to Hispaniola by Ovando in 1502, and they had adapted so well to the climate and were such strong workers that from about 1510 large numbers were shipped out each

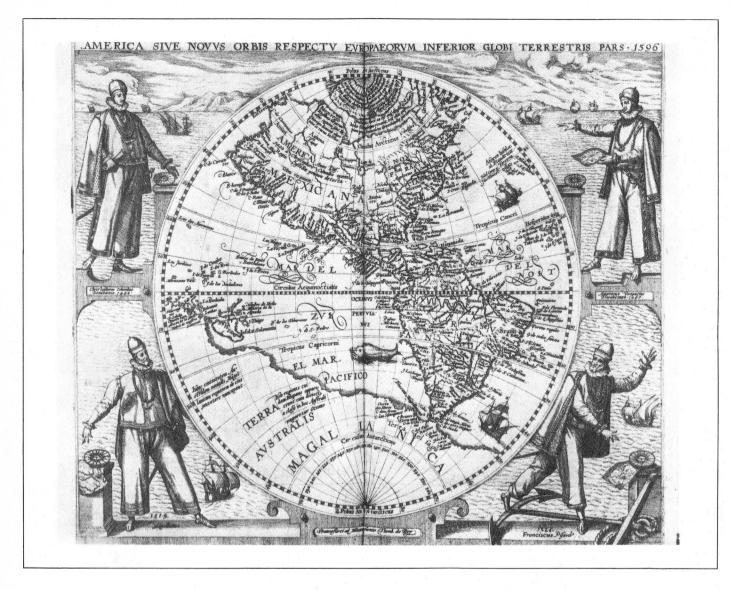

The western hemisphere as it was known – or imagined – at the end of the sixteenth-century. It is flanked by figures of Columbus, Vespucci, Magellan and Pizzarro.

year. The Indians, who had never made good slave labourers, were now no longer needed, and as a result whole populations were ruthlessly exterminated in the course of a few years.

Almost the only voice raised against this wanton destruction of a simple, gentle and peaceful people was that of Bartholomew de las Casas, who had accompanied Ovando to Hispaniola and in 1510 had been the first priest ordained in the New World. Las Casas devoted much of his life to exposing the inhumanities of his countrymen and to campaigning, with little success, for the more humane treatment of the wretched natives; and his *Historia de las Indias*, written late in his life but not printed until 1875, is a horrifying indictment of sixteenth century colonial rule.

The Spanish, he wrote, fell upon the harmless Indians 'as tigers, wolves and lions fall upon lambs and kids'. In forty years, he claimed, the native population of Hispaniola was reduced from an original 3,000,000 until 'barely three hundred remained to be counted', and

another 9,000,000 were just as ruthlessly slaughtered in Jamaica, Cuba and Puerto Rico.

'The lowest Spaniard could rape with impunity the wives and daughters of the highest chief,' he asserted, 'and for greed of gold many Indians were subjected to the most cruel tortures to force them to reveal the whereabouts of mines that did not exist'.

As cavaliers rode arrogantly through the streets of Santo Domingo, he declared, they made bets with each other as to who could cleave a passing native entirely with a single sweep, or who could run one through at a designated spot with sword or lance, and often a score would fall before a wager was won.

'Children were snatched from their mothers' arms and dashed against rocks or thrown into the water to drown,' he went on, 'and their bodies were thrown to the hounds to make them the more eager to catch their prey when hunting. A man could make no prouder boast of his hound than that it had killed or mangled half a thousand Indians.'

The Vision of Amerigo Vespucci, an allegorical engraving by Theodore de Bry.

Las Casas was, of course, essentially a propagandist and a passionate one, and historians are probably justified in dismissing some of his statements and statistics as exaggerations. The fact remains, however, that within half a century the population of the islands, whatever may have been their original number and the manner of their death, had almost ceased to exist; and basically the same was true when, having conquered the islands, the Spaniards turned their attention to the central and south American mainland.

Hardly a year passed without some new discovery or conquest. In 1513 Vasco Nuñez de Balboa, governor of the province of Darien, marched across the isthmus with a strong force and saw and named the Pacific Ocean. In the same year Ponce de Léon, in search of a fabulous island called Bimini where the fountain of eternal youth was said to flow, discovered and explored part of Florida, which he so named because of its variety of flowers and which he thought to be a very large island. Eight years later when attempting to colonize the place he was killed

by an Indian arrow. Balboa himself became a victim of intrigue. The complaints of his enemy, the incompetent Enciso, led to a charge of treason, and Balboa was executed in 1519.

As a result of Balboa's discovery of the Pacific, navigators were encouraged to seek a route to Asia around the southern tip of South America. In 1516, with this aim, a Spanish expedition under Juan Diaz de Solis reached as far south as the estuary of the River Plate on which were to rise the cities of Montevideo and Buenos Aires. However, Solis and some of his men were killed when they went ashore to parley with the local Indians, and the expedition was abandoned.

Three years later Ferdinand Magellan, a Portuguese who had entered the Spanish service, left Spain with five ships and about 270 men in the hope of succeeding where Solis had failed. The voyage was to become one of the most momentous in history. In 1520 Magellan discovered and sailed through the strait which separates the South American mainland from the island of Terra

below:
The Columbus memorial lighthouse, on the east
bank of the Ozama River, Santo Domingo, as it will
appear when completed. It is in the form of a cross,
set in a park of 2,500 acres, and will contain a
chapel with a tomb to hold Columbus's remains.
There will be side chapels, libraries and museums.
The design is by a Scottish architect, Joseph Lea
Gleave.

del Fuego and which still bears his name, and from there he continued on a north-westerly course across the Pacific to the Philippine Islands, which were soon afterwards claimed for Spain.

By this time most of his ships were rotting, many of his men had died from scurvy, and Magellan himself was killed in a pointless affray with some natives. However, one of his ships, the tiny *Vittoria*, continued on through the East Indies and around the Cape of Good Hope back to Spain, and the thirty-two survivors of her crew became the first men to circumnavigate the world.

By now Spanish eyes were on the mainland of America. In 1519, using Cuba as a base, Hernando Cortez invaded Mexico, and within a year he had conquered its Aztec inhabitants, imprisoned their king Montezuma who was later killed by his own people, and plundered and destroyed the Aztec capital. Tenochtitlán, which later became the site of Mexico City.

This was followed in 1522-24 by Pedro de Alvarado's conquest of Guatemala, which at that time comprised all Central America between Mexico and Panama, including the present republics of Nicaragua, Costa Rica and Honduras.

In 1532-33 another celebrated conquistador Francisco Pizarro, who had crossed the Isthmus with Balboa, invaded Peru, the centre of the great Inca civilization, executed the Inca king Atahualpa, replaced him with a puppet ruler, destroyed the ancient city of Cuzco and established a new capital called Lima. By 1535 Spaniards had begun to overrun Chile in search of gold, and within five years and in the face of fierce resistance the country had been conquered and a government under Pedro de Valdivia established. By this time Colombia was already under Spanish rule, and soon afterwards Venezuela was established as a captaincy-general.

Meanwhile King John III of Portugal had decided the time had come to colonize Brazil, which Portuguese and Spanish captains had been exploiting for twenty-five years or more for its valuable wood and other products. So that the cost of colonization would not be a burden on

the Crown the king divided the country into hereditary captaincies each with a coastal frontage of fifty leagues; and these he offered to people who were willing and able to establish permanent settlements. The first to take up the offer was Martin Affonso de Sousa, who discovered the site of Rio de Janeiro (the January River), on New Year's Day 1531 but chose instead to settle on the nearby island of São Vicente. Within another few years Pedro de Mendoza had established a Spanish settlement farther south at Buenos Aires on the Rio de la Plata which Vespucci had reached in 1501 and so laid the foundation of what is now Argentina.

Thus within half a century of Columbus's first historic voyage, most of the Caribbean Islands, the whole of Central America, and most of South America were firmly in Spanish or Portuguese hands, the world had been circumnavigated, and a westerly route to China and the East Indies had been opened. All these Columbus had made possible, and this was the real measure of his achievement.

It is ironic that within a year of Columbus's death, on the advocacy of an obscure German pedant who was deceived by the false claims of Amerigo Vespucci, the continent which surely should have borne Columbus's name was instead called America. Yet more modestly the name of Columbus still lives on – in the South American republic of Colombia, for instance; in the District of Columbia, U.S.A., in which the Federal capital of Washington stands; in the Canadian province of British Columbia; in several cities and towns of the United States including Columbus, Ohio; in the Columbia River, Oregon, in the University of Columbia, New York; and in Colón, the seaport at the eastern entrance to the Panama Canal, a waterway to the Pacific – and thence to Asia – where none existed in Columbus's day.

The United States and many Central and South American republics still celebrate as Columbus Day 12 October, the day on which, about five hundred years ago, the wool-weaver's son from Genoa first set foot on the soil of the New World.

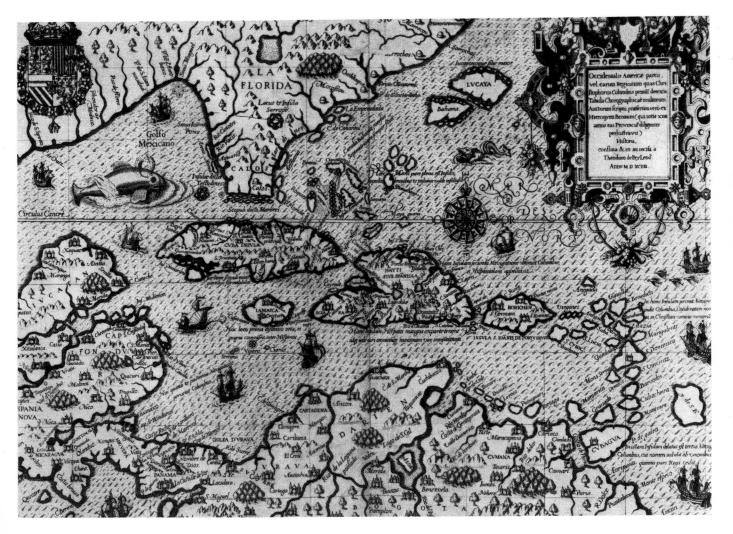

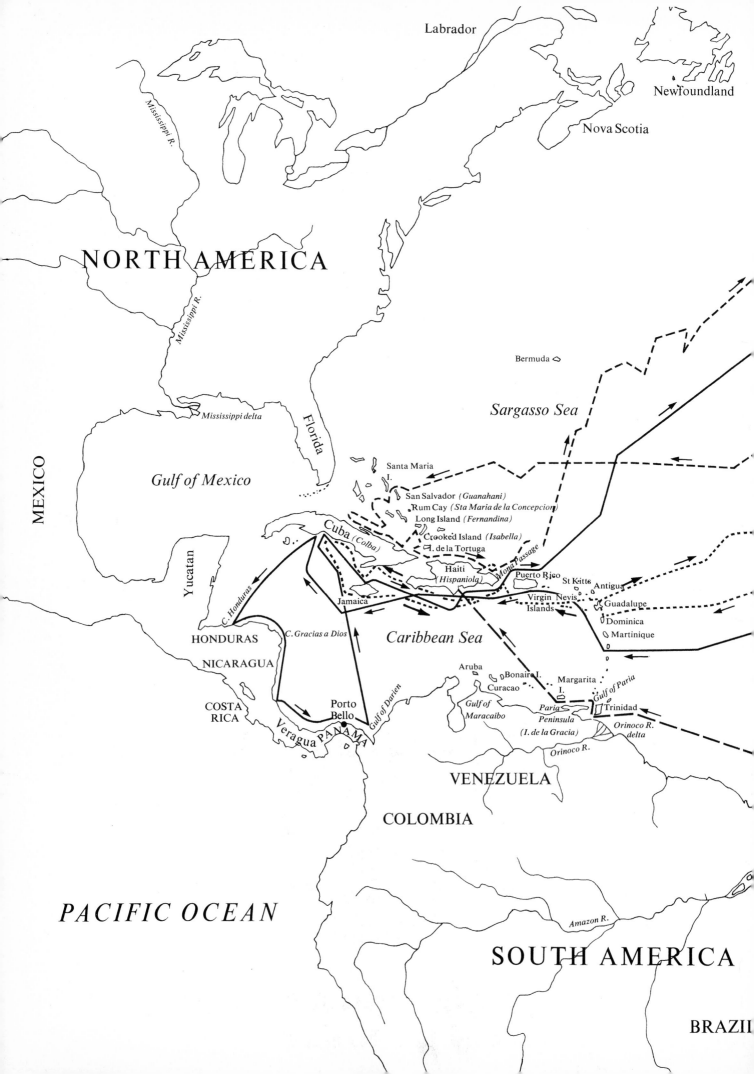

Labrador

Newfoundland

Nova Scotia

NORTH AMERICA

Mississippi R.

Mississippi R.

Bermuda

Sargasso Sea

MEXICO

Mississippi delta

Florida

Gulf of Mexico

Santa Maria I.

San Salvador *(Guanahani)*

Rum Cay *(Sta Maria de la Concepcion)*

Long Island *(Fernandina)*

Crooked Island *(Isabella)*

I. de la Tortuga

Cuba *(Colba)*

Haiti *(Hispaniola)*

Mona Passage

Puerto Rico

St Kitts

Antigua

Yucatan

Jamaica

Virgin Islands

Nevis

Guadalupe

Dominica

C. Honduras

HONDURAS

C. Gracias a Dios

Caribbean Sea

Martinique

NICARAGUA

COSTA RICA

Porto Bello

Gulf of Darien

Aruba

Curacao

Bonaire I.

Margarita I.

Gulf of Paria

Gulf of Maracaibo

Paria Peninsula (I. de la Gracia)

Trinidad

Veragua PANAMA

Orinoco R. delta

Orinoco R.

VENEZUELA

PACIFIC OCEAN

COLOMBIA

Amazon R.

SOUTH AMERICA

BRAZIL

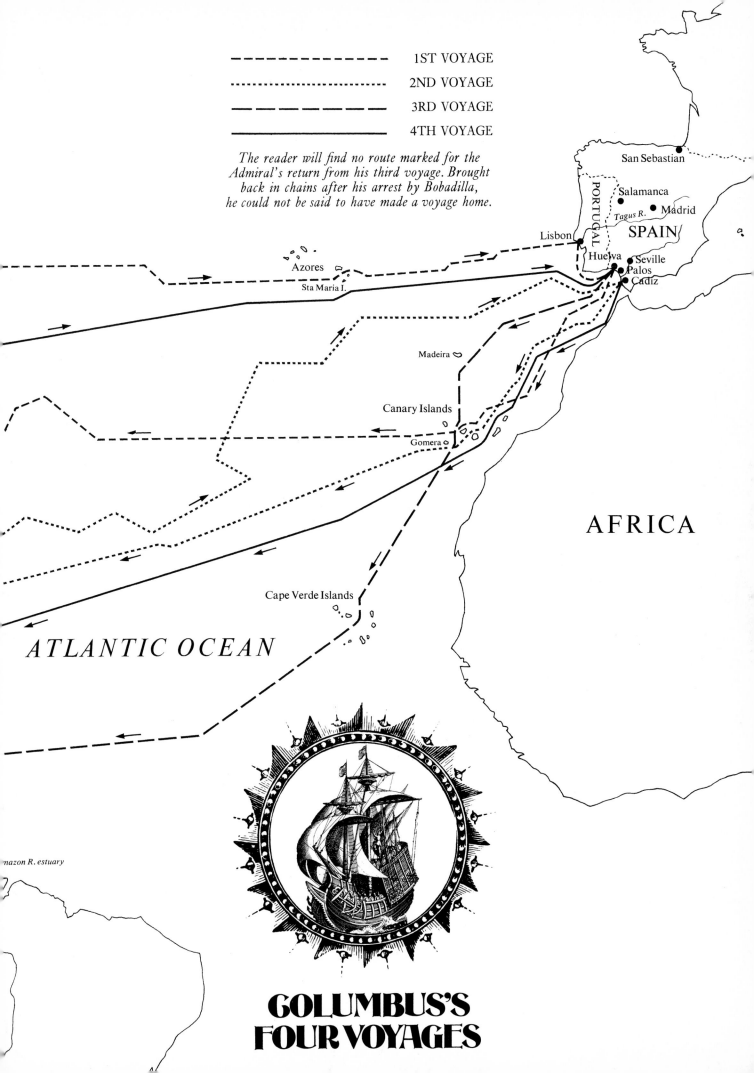

1ST VOYAGE

2ND VOYAGE

3RD VOYAGE

4TH VOYAGE

The reader will find no route marked for the Admiral's return from his third voyage. Brought back in chains after his arrest by Bobadilla, he could not be said to have made a voyage home.

San Sebastian

Salamanca

PORTUGAL · *Tagus R.* · Madrid

SPAIN

Lisbon

Huelva · Seville · Palos · Cadiz

Azores

Sta Maria I.

Madeira

AFRICA

Canary Islands

Gomera

Cape Verde Islands

ATLANTIC OCEAN

mazon R. estuary

GOLUMBUS'S FOUR VOYAGES

FURTHER READING LIST

Brebner, J. B. *Explorers of North America.* New York, 1955
Burland, Cottie *The People of the Ancient Americas.* London, 1970
Collis, Maurice *Marco Polo.* London, 1950
    Cortés and Montezuma. London, 1954
Columbus, Christopher *The Journals* (trans. by Cecil Jane). Cambridge, 1960
De Madariaga, Salvador *Christopher Columbus.* Connecticut, 1979
Díaz, Bernal *The Conquest of New Spain* (trans. by J. M. Cohen). Harmondsworth, 1963
Duff, Charles *The Truth about Columbus.* London, 1936
Granzotto, Gianni *Christopher Columbus.* New York, 1985
Hagen, Victor W. von *The Ancient Sun Kingdoms.* London, 1962
Haring, C. H. *The Spanish Empire in America.* Oxford, 1947
Helps, Arthus *The Life of La Casas, the Apostle of the Indies.* London, 1868
Howarth, David *The Golden Isthmus.* London, 1966
Jones, G. *The Norse Atlantic Saga.* Oxford, 1964
Keen, Benjamin *The Life of the Admiral Christopher Columbus by his son Ferdinand.* New Jersey, 1959
Landström, Björn *Columbus.* London, 1967
Morison, S. E. *Christopher Columbus, Admiral of the Ocean Sea.* Oxford, 1942
Nowell, C. E. *Great Discoveries and the First Colonial Empires.* Minneapolis, 1954
Parry, J. H. *The Age of Reconnaissance.* London, 1963
Prescott, William H. *History of the Reigns of Ferdinand and Isabella the Catholic.* Liverpool, 1962
Prestage, Edgar *The Portuguese Pioneers.* London, 1933
Skelton, R. A. *Explorers' Maps.* London, 1958
Stanley, Henry E. J. *The Three Voyages of Vasco de Gama and his Viceroyalty.* London, 1869
Törnae, J. K. P. *Norsemen before Columbus.* London, 1966
Tschiffely, A. S. *Coricancha.* London, 1949
Williamson, James A. *The Cabot Voyages and Bristol Discovery under Henry VII.* Glasgow, 1962

ACKNOWLEDGMENTS

The publishers gratefully acknowledge the following sources for permission to use the illustrations indicated.

COLOR
Bodleian Library, Oxford: 19, 26 lower, 27. Bologna University Library: 87 upper. Civico Museo Archaeologico, Como: 18. Hamlyn Group Library: 51 lower. Michael Holford-Hamlyn Group Library: 23, 87 lower, 90 lower, 134 upper. Mansell Collection: 30. Mariners' Museum Virginia: 50, 51 upper, 54 upper, 58 upper, 90 upper. Arnoldo Mondadori Co. Ltd: 26 upper, 55, 91, 134 lower. National Gallery of Art, Washington: 31 lower, 54 lower, 59 lower. National Maritime Museum: 58 lower, 59 upper. National Portrait Gallery: 86, 94, 95. Ship Museum, Oslo: 22. Enrico Polidori: 130-31. Museo del Prado, Madrid: 31 upper. Constantino Reyes Valerio-Hamlyn Group Library: 135. Henri Stierlin: 138-9.

BLACK & WHITE
British Museum: 8, 13, 14, 20, 24, 25, 28, 42 upper, 34, 45 upper, 46-7, 48, 49, 52, 53, 56, 65, 66 left, 67, 69, 70, 71, 72, 73, 74, 75, 76-7, 79, 80-81, 85, 93, 96, 97, 98-9, 100, 101, 102, 103, 104, 105, 106-7, 108-9, 113, 114-5, 116, 117, 118-9, 120-1, 122-3, 124 right, 126 upper, 129, 132 lower, 133, 144, 145, 147. Brown Brothers, N.Y.: 39. Central office of Information, London: 78. Copenhagen National Museum: 10 upper. Embassy of the Dominican Republic: 132 upper, 146. Alfred Gregory: 11. A. F. Kersting: 32. Mansell Collection: 33, 45 lower, 66 right, 88-9, 92, 126 lower, 136, 137, 140, 141. Mariners' Museum, Virginia: 40, 41. Foto Mas, Barcelona: 7, 36, 37, 42 lower, 43, 44, 57, 61, 68, 111, 128. Arnoldo Mondadori Co. Ltd: 112. Musée de l'Homme: 10 lower. Museum of Primitive Art: 124 left. National Gallery of Art, Washington: 35 lower. Perestrello, Madeira: 16 upper. Portuguese State Office: 15, 16 lower, 35 upper. Roger Viollet: 32, 60. United States Information Service: 9.

INDEX